BLACK NAMES

Contributions to the Sociology Language

13

Joshua A. Fishman
Editor

MOUTON · THE HAGUE · PARIS

Black Names

J. L. Dillard

MOUTON · THE HAGUE · PARIS

ISBN: 90 279 7602 3
Cover design by Jurriaan Schrofer
© 1976, Mouton & Co., Publishers, The Hague
Printed in the Netherlands

Contents

Contents

Introduction: The Problem of Black Names

To the student of non-standard language varieties, names may have a special significance. Like the language varieties themselves the names which the speakers characteristically use may be passed off as insignificant, even haphazard deviations from the prestigious norm – in effect, 'performance errors'. It is even denied, occasionally, that either the names or the language varieties 'exist';[1] it is asserted that the observer has either invented or imagined radically non-standard grammatical structures[2] or that he has hallucinated a vehicle bearing an exotic name. The very existence of the naming pattern may, then, be a vexed empirical question, just as the existence of a variety like Black English[3] may be highly controversial even insofar as the data for analysis are concerned.

The question of Afro-American names abuts on another issue of both empirical and theoretical importance. It has been claimed by a great many anthropologists, folklorists, sociologists, etc.,[4] that African cultural patterns died out completely in the early years of slavery, that Black slaves became rather gruesome 'carbon copies' of their European masters. A great deal of idealistically liberal thought is predicated upon this assumption,[5] but there are some indications that liberalism would be more effective if founded upon sounder historical facts. Such issues as prostitution, compensation, and even welfare seem hardly to have any direct relevance to the question as to whether the slaves were at some early stage reduced to non-human or semi-human status. In fact, American slavery was no unusual institution on the entire scale of history, and the question of cultural survivals in the context of even such a degrading status may have importance and application for a number of other historical situations.

The rueful side of Black-white and slave-master relationships is, of course, also reflected in the naming practices. As many observers, including the anonymous author of 'Word Shadows'[6] observed, slaves on the U.S. plantations named cornbread 'John Constant', wheat bread 'Billy Seldom'. For some not quite so obvious reason, bacon was 'Ole Ned'. Analogous to such designations is the development of a terminology to express shades of skin color (Johnson 1973), whereby resentment can be expressed and control of the process, by even the most domineering master, is virtually impossible. Even from evidence of this sort, we can hardly avoid the conclusion that naming patterns in the New World were not altogether white-imposed.

The study of African cultural survivals in the New World is an old one, having its most notable statement in the works of Herskovits in the 1940's.[7] Conclusions derived from this kind of research cannot be considered hackneyed, however, since the dissemination of the results has not been especially wide. In fact, a great many researchers in major disciplines have simply ignored the implications of the Herskovitsian tradition. As dialectologists[8] still unquestioningly start to trace English forms elicited primarily or solely from Negro informants back to some 'regional' dialect of British English, so some folklorists automatically exclude thoughts of African origin or special transmission from their formulations about folk tales and other aspects of culture collected from Black informants. It has even been asserted that the learning of the English language by Blacks excluded their retaining any African patterns:

> ... we submit two factors greatly influencing the assimilation of European occult beliefs by eighteenth-century Negroes. These factors were the language spoken by the Negroes and the church attended by them.[9]

The same author continues:

> Everywhere English became the accepted method of communication and English folk beliefs and superstitions were given an enormous advantage over the African forms.[10]

Pointing out the assimilatory influence of the church, Whitten states further:

> Communicating with English symbols, and attending an institution devoted to explaining and justifying the real and supernatural, Ne-

groes in the context of a close contact situation dominated by whites, assimilated a body of occult beliefs and practices more European than African in character.[11]

Whitten thus joins the issue of language to that of folklore and culture in general – making an issue which every researcher in Afro-American language and culture has long been eager to confront. This 'close contact' explanation, assuming white historical dominance, is equally a lively issue. It has been invoked by that school of dialectology which asserts that Black English Vernacular cannot exist, and that essentially British dialect distribution dominates American English.[12] For rebuttal, see my *All-American English* (1975).

Whitten, like many others with his orientation, invokes against African influence in the 'English symbol system' by which beliefs were purportedly conveyed to the Negroes the double defense that
1) few words can be traced to African origin;
2) even those which can be traced are limited to Gullah, which is spoken by a small minority of American Negroes.

Against this may be presented two arguments:
1) that of Dalby (1972);
2) that of the American 'creolists' who have concerned themselves with the Black English vernacular.

Dalby shows convincingly that individual words do not constitute the only contribution of 'Africanism' and that the kinds of phrasal expressions *(big eye, bad mouth)* for which he finds African origins are not uniquely characteristic of Black speech but have also spread to white Americans. Probably the most significant Africanism in American English, *O.K.*, is often mistaken for some weird kind of pseudo-acronym. The creolists (Stewart 1967, 1968; Dillard 1972) have insisted that the surface forms (etymology) of the words tell less historically than the grammatical structures of the speech of American Negroes of the socio-economic class often stigmatized as 'disadvantaged' (and formed largely of the descendants of plantation field hands who were the ones who spoke Plantation Creole).

Indeed, in the words of Stewart (personal communication) it is not – either in language or in culture – the 'bits and pieces' that count but the pattern. If a lot of British occult beliefs – even an overwhelming majority of the items – are shaped into an 'African' pattern, then 'Africanism' is a very prominent factor in such beliefs. In fact, it could properly be said to dominate that belief system. Further, the assumption of white domination in the contact situation has been effectively challenged. Genovese's *Roll, Jordan, Roll* (1974) and Wood's *Black Majority* (1974) are indicative of a new trend among historians of slavery. Even Genovese's subtitle *The World the Slaves Made*, a significant alteration of his earlier *The World the Slaveholders Made*, emphasizes how some historians are no longer looking only at the official surface but are delving beneath. Under the surface, a great deal of Black influence can be found. In fact, Wood shows how the South Carolina colony would hardly have survived without its Black slaves and how their skill in rice cultivation and cattle raising was of basic importance to the later prosperity of the colony.

The opposite temptation to assuming purely European influence is the temptation to find a too direct influence from Africa. This temptation, I believe, has been most successfully avoided by the American 'creolists'. Seldom is it possible to trace a feature to Africa, especially to a given area or tribe, with any confidence. Despite some optimism and some downright folklore,[13] tribal and regional origins of the slaves have been largely inaccessible throughout the duration of the Blacks' originally enforced stay in the Americas.[14]

Fortunately, neither horn of the dilemma is all that inescapable. The reconstructionists (certainly in linguistics) have consistently placed unnecessary limitations on historical work by insisting upon tracing the origin in *regional* varieties of the originally European languages. This is, of course, the unfortunate but perfectly natural outcome of the early emphases of the internal reconstructionists.[15] The Africanists, on the other hand, have looked to the kinds of groups studied by the classical (nineteenth century) anthropologists – tribal groups which are as nearly 'pure' or 'unspoiled' as possible, as far out of contact with Europeans as possible.

The basic issue is well put by one of the most distinguished investigators of Afro-American culture, Richard Price:

> ... maroons could and did look to Africa for deep-level organizational principles, relating to cultural realms as diverse as naming their children on the one hand, or systems of justice on the other.[16]

Price is not completely on the side of the angels in this argument. He asserts that 'other Afro-Americans were unable to pass on integrated patterns of traditional culture'. In the post-Herskovitsian tradition, this

.ient is controversial if not positively heretical. But Price is ob-
right in looking for *deep-level* rather than superficial principles.
unately for the investigation (if not for the population!) contact
uropeans is a widespread fact in West Africa – almost as much
n the New World – and contact conditions comparable to those
very and early Emancipation are to some degree observable. In-
as these circumstances have been treated in the literature, they
been dealt with under the heading of acculturation.[17] Fortunately,
.it deal of the work on acculturation, while almost by definition
iventional, has been of very high grade. The researcher who wishes
ncern himself with non-traditional topics has a lot of high-level
anionship and guidance from those researchers into the accultura-
process. The work of scholars like Parrinder (1953) on West
an religious syncretism and of Simpson (1965) on the same factors
e West Indies has provided an incalculable boost for this study.
there is always the indispensable work of Herskovits and his immediate associates.

In the case of onomastic studies, the researcher into Black names
finds himself casting his lot with those out-of-the-mainstream students
of acculturation or else withdrawing from the field. Naming studies, as
shown for example from typical articles in periodicals like the American *Names*,[18] tend to be almost exclusively devoted to place names.
British (like other European) place name studies have been based on
the model of displacement of the more or less original owners of the
land (the Celts) by invaders (the Anglo-Saxons), with later overlays
(Norman French), etc. In a rather subservient manner, American onomastics has merely substituted American Indians for Celts and Europeans for Anglo-Saxons. The Blacks, who never owned more than a
small portion of the land and who never placed either conquering or
defeated armies in the field, can hardly be compared to the Celts or
the Norman French in their influence on place names. The usual conclusion has been that Blacks had no great influence on American
naming patterns.

If we look at the informal naming patterns, rather than official patterns which form the exclusive material of most studies, we find some
modification of that viewpoint. Genovese (1974: 448) cites Duncan
Clinch Heyward's report that:

It was one thing for 'Ole Maussah' . . . to give his plantations such names [Rotterdam, Amsterdam, etc.] and quite another to get his Negroes to call them by these names.

According to Heyward, the slaves changed the names to 'De Swamp' and 'De Lower Swamp'. Furthermore, Heyward reports that "these names stuck in spite of 'Ole Maussuh' ".

Even from the extreme case of official place names in the continental United States, there cannot be complete exclusion of Black influence. There is Cudjo Key in Florida, Gumbo Springs (where the first word is an acknowledged Africanism) in Virginia, and occasional other names which bring the reaction:

I had lived all my early years near a well-known landmark called *Cudjo's Cave* without knowing that Cudjo is an African day name for a male born on Monday.[19]

In the West Indies, Black influence on even the place names produces occasionally spectacular results. Even David DeCamp, a severely formal linguist when describing Jamaican Creole, is moved to write when dealing with Jamaican names:

Jamaicans enjoy naming things. The place names of Jamaica are a source of onomastic delight: e.g., Maggotty Pen, Look Behind, Corn-Puss Gap, Me no Sen' You no Come, Half Way Tree.[20]

One is tempted to add other names like Gimme Me Bit, Clarendon,[21] the picturesqueness of which is not much affected by the knowledge that 'Gimme Me Bit' is the name (allegedly onomatopoetic) of a bird.

The same 'joy' in naming places could be said to have worked in other Caribbean islands. On St. Croix in the Virgin Islands we find place names like All for the Better and Profit. These are not unusual for the island. In fact, there are so many of them that they have attracted the attention of tourists:

Places are called Upper Love, Lower Love, Jealously, Dot's Folly, Hannah Rest, Judiths's Fancy,[22] Bethlehem, Slob.[23]

Observers often apply adjectives like 'balmy' and 'Oz-like' to such names, and speculate about their 'Danish' influence. But, since similar names are to be found in the West Indian islands with no conceivable influence from Danish (e.g., Jamaica), it is much more likely that the Black populations of the islands are responsible for the pattern.

In Paramaribo, Surinam, the old native market is known as Puru Pangi '[place where one can] Pull [off] the Loincloth'. Psychologizers, who rush in eagerly where conventional name researchers have feared to tread, can easily find these 'fascinating names which today would raise a Freudian eyebrow'.[24] The truth is, however, more mundane. In the case of Puru Pangi, it relates rather to the Creole eagerness to be free from the irksome apparel requirements of a different culture with different dress styles than to any revelations which would have been of great interest to Sigmund Freud.

In other cases, anyway, the names are considerably more prosaic. A good case is what the West Indian English-speaking residents of St. John call the side away from White Bay – Terra Side 'the other side'. Whether through any possible historical connection or not, Willemstad, Curaçao, names its newer and more modern sector Otrabanda 'the other side'. (Translation relationships of the same type are striking in Pidgin and Creole studies: Pidgin English *husay* and French Creole *ki kote* 'where?'). Nevertheless, the place names of the West Indies – and other kinds of Black names in the continental United States – are of a type to motivate writers to talk of the 'joy of naming' and to invoke adjectives like *peppery* and *salty*.

Many of these treatments have been casual, even to the point of irresponsibility. Such professionals as have concerned themselves with the matter have not necessarily done better than newspaper reporters.[25] Perhaps the first to undertake any serious work of an explanatory nature was G. Thomas Fairclough. His discussion of the 'secular' content of white Baptist church names in New Orleans as against the 'religious' emphases in the Black church names of the same denomination in the same city seems to constitute a landmark in such studies.

Others have had similar impressions of different aspects of Black onomastics. DeCamp's discussion of the 'joy' Jamaicans take in naming (quoted above) represents the kind of perception, despite its lacks of formality and perhaps of susceptibility to objective demonstration, which might perhaps be synthesized with that of Fairclough.

According to DeCamp, there are three main categories of Jamaican cart names:

1) names derived from other names (of places, persons, political parties, etc.);
2) names derived from topics in current events;

3) newly-created names which express the personal mood or aspirations of the owner.[26]

As DeCamp points out, these categories frequently overlap. As a matter
of fact, if categories (2) and (3) were combined into one category like
newly-created names which derive from events in the life of the person
and/or express his personal mood or aspirations, there would probably
be accomplished a near epitome of what is peculiar to Afro-American
naming patterns. (See, especially, Chapters 1 and 3 below.)

In the absence of the empathy with the group which derives from
personal experience or of in-depth investigation, however, some kind
of polarity like Fairclough's secular/religious is needed to explain the
feeling of distinctive 'Blackness' which is frequently the intuitive reaction to some of the naming patterns. Reactions frequently run to terms
of this sort:

Black	*White*
religious or spiritual	secular
innovative	stereotyped
culture-oriented	geography-oriented[27]
figurative	literal
allusive	scholiastic
periphrastic	metaphrastic

Trying to retain the valuable suggestion by Fairclough but to extend
it into a wider domain, I have decided to utilize for the final sum-
marizing designations

White	*Black*
Labeling	Expressive

I hope that the materials contained in the chapters to follow will sub-
stantiate the claim that such designations have explanatory value.

A small girl in the fifth grade in St. John, responding to a routine
Language Arts classroom exercise, produced a very non-routine story
about some ponies, illustrated by a magnificent drawing of one big-
maned pony. Within the story, she named one group of two ponies (or,
as she wrote it, *to pony*)[28] Toney-bow-loney and Stick-up-lar-Porker.
Later a third was introduced, Cotton-lar-Porker. Several native St.
Johnians, including at least one professional linguist, have struggled
with explaining to me, but all admit that they cannot really plumb the
depths of the little girl's imagination. We all feel, however, that the

names say a lot about the naming facility which the little girl and all her schoolmates have.

Reiterating the principle of this linguistic facility can perhaps never be overdone. There are always cases like that of Fader (1971), who carefully explains how the title *The Naked Children* refers to a linguistic nakedness and who never seems quite to make up his mind whether their nonstandard dialect constitutes such nakedness or not. Fader continually flirts, as do many other such investigators, with the threadbare theory of linguistic deprivation (see Deutsch 1964), and not even the fact that his ghetto students have a great deal of creativity (as partly illustrated by such nicknames as Rubbergut, for a little boy who can eat anything) dissuades him from that theory entirely.

It is idle to think that either *Rubbergut* or *Toney-bow-loney* will ever be explained by a search through African language dictionaries and an identification of the West African source.[29] So to assume would be to underestimate woefully the innovative powers of the people who gave or assumed such names. But to make the even more facile assumption that environmental influences somehow determined the names, or that they were all copied from whites, would surely be worse. We are left, I feel, with the unglamorous but necessary task of trying to explain in a reasonable way what models there were for innovations of names and how transmissions took place or may plausibly have taken place. If this does not constitute the ultimate in explanatory theories, it seems at least to be a necessary condition for any explanatory theory which can be seriously developed and defended.

1. Personal Names

Within the past few years, the most overtly obvious and self-conscious manifestation of Black naming practices has attracted a great deal of attention within the United States. Kohl and Hinton (1972) report how Harlem youngsters who have taken for themselves names (or nicknames) like Akmir, Arkbar, and Rabu have 'recently discovered Africa – not the Africa of the school textbooks, the white man's burden, but a proud continent with a complex cultural history'. On July 29, 1968, *Newsweek*, the popular weekly magazine, ran an article 'Black Names', calling attention to how, as 'Black consciousness becomes more widespread' many Blacks are looking away from former naming practices and 'looking elsewhere for a more relevant identity'. Much of the material written on this subject concerned itself with how Blacks were giving up 'slave' names and turning to Muslim names, under the influence of the Black Muslim movement. They reported, for new births in Detroit, such names as Satonya, Djuna, Gernon, Narda, Tyeise Luhema, Muhammed Sharieff, and Attallah ('gift of God'). The last was given to his new-born daughter by a Black American with the quite prosaically American name of Edward Vaughn. As the *Newsweek* article pointed out, many of these names combine African languages like Xhosa and Swahili in Thanayi Anane ('child of happiness' and 'soft and gentle'), Tiyor Siyolo (Sutu and Zulu words for 'wise one' and 'bringer of happiness'), Tarik Saidi (Arabic and Swahili for 'he who splits his enemies' and 'Lord').

The purist could find objection to these practices all too easily: Xhosa and Swahili are well known to be spoken essentially outside the areas from which any large numbers of slaves were taken, and historically this onomastic searching for roots looked rather embarrassingly like the pseudo-Ethiopianism which had long afflicted Black movements like the Jamaican Ras Tafari.[1] Like the country of Ethiopia, Swahili is an important symbol of Africa to the outside – and, being a Bantu language, it is far from unrelated to the languages which many of the slaves must have spoken – but it is (now at least) an essentially East and Central rather than West African phenomenon.

On a broader scale, Black apologists could give a better account of themselves than simply misapplied history. 'Going back to the roots' – looking for historical authenticity – was only a small part of what the Black parent wished to express when he gave his child an African name, be it Swahili, Zulu, Xhosa, Arabic, or whatever. There was also, as pointed out in the *Newsweek* article, a great emphasis on the names of Africans who were becoming of world importance as the 'winds of freedom' stirred the 'dark' continent: Kenyan President Jomo Kenyatta, Congo revolutionary Patrice Lumumba, President Julius Nyerere of Tanzania, and ex-President Kwame Nkrumah of Ghana. Perhaps the average Black parent who named his child Kwame was unaware that the name means 'Saturday' – that it is the name for a male child born on that day of the week and therefore one of the well-known day names.[2] But the superficial inadvertence could not completely mask the significance of a recurrent pattern: Whatever their rationale for doing so, Black Americans were once again giving their children a name which had been given in Africa before the slave trade, which was given during the slave trade, and which survived well into the periods of slavery and Emancipation.[3]

There were other names, however, which belonged to that same tradition and which remained in continuous use from the time of West Africans' being carried from their homeland to the New World as slaves. All fourteen of the day names figured in that process. Newbell Niles Puckett's pioneering article (1937) established the principle that

> The African practice of naming a child according to the day of the week on which he was born persisted in Jamaica, and a number of these traditional Jamaican names are found in the United States, e.g., Quashe, Cudjo, Quaco, and Cuffee among the male slaves and Juba, Beneva, Cooba (spelled Cubah or Cubbah) and Abba (spelled Abah) among female slaves.

Subsequent research (Cassidy 1961; DeCamp 1967) has been more completely revealing of the Jamaican day name pattern,[4] and other research (Dillard 1971, 1972) has shown that Jamaica is no such special case in the areas where there is an Afro-American population. Furthermore, Price and Price (1972) and others have shown or at least suggested strongly how much more completely the African processes may be reflected in Surinam, where assimilation to the white man's cultural processes is less than elsewhere in the New World and even in some parts of Africa – as reflected in the relatively slight decreolization[5] of the English-based varieties Sranan Tongo, Djouka, and Saramaccan.[6]

In earlier times, the day-naming practices were certainly part of slave culture in the United States – and by no means exclusively in the Sea Islands where Gullah (also called 'Geechee') was spoken. Dillard (1972: 123–135) shows how such names were used outside Gullah territory, Wood (1974: 181) cites the statement with approval, and Genovese (1975: 448) reports that

> The slaves of the South Carolina and Georgia low country never gave up this practice, which echoed across the South.

Finding the day names, relatively unaltered, in the plantation records is an easy matter; those who haven't found them simply haven't looked. There are, it is true, some disguising practices which add complexity to the problem. On the other hand, it becomes a more interesting problem because of them. Wood agrees with my statement in *Black English*:

> One regular compromise was to accept a direct English translation: Negroes were called *Monday* or *Friday*, as well as other temporal names such as *March* and *August, Christmas* and *Midday.*

Evidence for the translation of the day names is everywhere in the historical records of slavery, and Nigerians and Cameroonians named Monday and Friday are fairly easy to meet in West Africa today.[7] The expansion process indicated in *March, Christmas*, etc., is even more important, since it enables us to begin seeing how superficially dissimilar patterns, which might be thought to be unrelated, developed out of the clearly African practices. Virtually every Southerner can cite examples like Aunt Easter, from Nacogdoches, Texas, in the 1930's.[8]

The day names proper were early exposed to some of the same kinds of disguising processes. As Genovese (1974: 448–449) puts it:

> A slave named Quack would be taken by white travelers to be the victim of some master's bad taste, but probably his own parents had

simply adapted the African Quaco, meaning a male born on Wednesday. A woman named Squash probably got her name from Quashee – a female born on Sunday. Actually, Quashee is a male day name. The common name Cuffee suggests both a male born on Friday and the Ashanti name Kofi. Some variation of Phoebe might look like a master's fancy, but Phiba or Phibbi means a female born on Friday. . . .

Furthermore, according to Genovese:

In time, the slaves anglicized these African names in their own way. Thus, Cudjo might become Monday in one generation and Joe in the next; Quaco might become Wednesday but sooner or later would end up as Jacco, Jacky, or Jack. If a master wanted to name a slave Hercules, the slave parents might think it a fine idea, for *heke* means 'large wild animal' in Mende. Cato suggests several perfectly good West African names, whatever the master may have intended (p. 449).

Wood (1974: 183), who also cites Mende *heke* for 'the name Hercules – often pronounced and spelled *Hekles*', cites *Keta* (Bambara, Yoruba, and Hausa) as being similar to Cato, and Mende *Haga* 'lazy' as being like the very frequent slave name Hagar.

Genovese's work, like Wood's and my own in *Black English*, tends to be somewhat concentrated in the American South, but the same kind of detective work will show strikingly similar patterns in the Northern colonies and even in areas north of the United States. Day names in the Northern colonies were recorded (although he did not so identify them) in Greene's (1942) important study of *The Negro in Colonial New England*. Investigation of the language and culture of the Black population of Nova Scotia, where slaves were to be found as early as 1750, shows very much the same patterns as those found in the United States. The extension of the day names was in fact as great as that of the Pidgin English which clearly underlies the history of the variety now called Black English Vernacular and of the English-based Creoles (Stewart 1967, 1968; Dillard 1972).

Through the orthographic flaws and variants of the records of slave sales and shipments which survive, it is possible to find a substantial number of such names even in a supposedly unlikely place like Halifax. The two most prevalent day names in these records are Quaco 'Wednesday (male)' and Quashee 'Sunday (male)'. In C. G. Fergusson's archive materials (1948), we can find two occurrences of Quack (p. 93: Quack Mantle and Quack Cooper), four of Quashy (p. 97: Quashy Cooper, Sr., Quashy Hamilton; Quashy Mantle; Quashy Cooper, Jr.). There are two occurrences of the shortened form *Quash* (p. 93: Quash Cooper; p. 102: Quash Cooper), probably referring to either Quashy Cooper, Sr., or to Quashy Cooper, Jr., the same men listed on p. 97. Obviously, -*y* for -*ee* poses no problem, since orthographic practices for slave day names were hardly standardized. In spite of Genovese's comment about 'some master's bad taste', the shortened form *Quack* for *Quaco* may represent a slave's partial assimilation to English, a language in which final -*o* is not common in proper names.

The anglicizing tendencies, as Genovese suggests, are persistent and impressive. To understand them, however, we must take into account more than has been previously allowed for about the history of the variety of English spoken by the slaves. As in Genovese's records, so there are examples of *Squash* in those cited by Fergusson (p. 102). A likely reason is that English-speaking whites kept the records. Familiar with Pidgin English phonological reduction of initial *sp-*, *st-*, *sk-* clusters, a slave owner might well assume that a slave who identified himself as *Quash* was 'trying to say' *Squash*. ('Quashee peakee', not improbable Pidgin English for 'Quashee speaks', would be hypercorrected by the white keeping records to 'Squash speaks'.)[9] For the use of Pidgin English in the Nova Scotian slave community, see Dillard (1973).

Another way to handle the day names, within a framework of limited acculturation — in Nova Scotia as elsewhere – was to translate them. Such translation, as Genovese suggests, must have been done by the slaves themselves, since there is no indication that any whites understood the pattern well enough to perform the translations. Fergusson has a Monday Bold (p. 81) and a Phoebe Cooper. The latter is an example of the fine line – unimportant, of course, to either the slave or the owner, both of whom were more or less intent upon acculturation – between translation and phonetic adaptation. The processes, however, were Nova Scotian as well as Southern. Believing that some of the slave women were named for the goddess of the moon, whites apparently proceeded to the next logical step and gave names like Caesar (the name most frequently cited in the materials gathered by Fergusson). That name, like the equally familiar Scipio, goes through enough variations in spelling to make us doubt that the owners and traders were such classicists as to be likely to conceive of such naming practices without the impetus of a (misunderstood) West African naming tradition. The latter name is still used in the Black community today: William A. Stewart has told me of a boy named Scipio whom he met in South Carolina, and there is a Scipio Spinks who pitched in the major leagues.

As Puckett carefully pointed out, the survival of African names was no mere matter of quaint archaism. He cites Cobb,[10] who reported on four native Africans among the Georgia slave community whose names were Capity, Saminy, Quominy, and Quor, who had such typically African cultural patterns as facial tattooing, and who 'were treated with marked respect by all the other Negroes for miles and miles around'. Puckett also pointed out that the 'African captions may have conferred a certain amount of distinction among the slaves' and he referred to the fact that the 'free Negroes of 1830 seem to have possessed a larger assortment of African names than did the slaves of that period'.[11] As Antiguan Milford A. Jeremiah puts it: 'These kinds of coping mechanisms were expressed through the unwillingness of slaves to change their African names or severely modify other aspects of culture'.[12] Those who held on to their African identity may also have been the ones who were bolder in opposition to white dominance. There is a preponderance of day names among the leaders of the very early slave revolts.[13] Leaders of the Jamaican Maroons in 1738 included, according to Price, Captain Cudjoe, Captain Accompong, Captain Cuffee, Captain Quaco, and only one 'secularly' named leader – Captain Johnny.

In the Northern United States and elsewhere, other patterns which have a much better chance of being African than European have been at least sporadically reported. Greene's important but generally over-looked *The Negro in Colonial New England* (1942) recorded a Boston Ken who was called Bus Bus (p. 316), and the most elementary study of West African and Afro-Creole patterns will reveal the tendency to reduplications. Listeners to the Nigerian radio may recall a program 'Save Journey' (about an eponymous bus and its drivers) whose principal character had the official name Shakespeare but the sobriquet Shaky Shaky. A student recorded such forms as Momo (for a girl whose baptismal name had been Mona Lisa), She She (for Sheila), and Lee Lee (for Lisa) for me in Bedford, Virginia, as late as 1967. (Another girl in the same group was named E Pluribus Unum and nicknamed Penny.)[14]

Surnames might, of course, have been harder to adapt to any African patterns. Genovese shows, however, how the simple pattern of the slave's taking his master's name was not always followed:

> With freedom, many Blacks took particular surnames for reasons other than to establish a historical link with their own family, especially since it was often difficult or impossible to do so. At the very least, they wanted the privilege of selecting a name and thereby establishing their right to make a choice. In some cases, they were resorting to a ruse. . . . Others were seeking protection. By reaching for the name of a big and respected planter, they hoped to enlist his sympathy should trouble come . . . (1975: 447).

But the more independent ex-slaves very quickly established a pattern later to become the hallmark of Black militancy in names (cf. Imamu Amiri Baraka). Ex-slaves with a greater sense of independence might follow different patterns. Shipping magnate Paul Cuffe (once known as Cuffee Slocum, when owned by a man named Slocum) is an outstanding example of how the day names became surnames in some cases. De Granda (1971) cites another distinguished example in Philip Quaque, first pastor of the Black race on the Gold Coast.

Today, the day names as surnames are more frequent than a few people (like Elsdon Smith, author of *American Surnames*) suspect. In the Manhattan telephone book for New York City, to cite only the most obvious example, there are fourteen entries for the surname *Cuff* (a frequent form of the day name in the records of slavery) and nine of *Cuffe*, *Cuffee*, and *Cuffie*. The addresses of nearly all of them are in Harlem. The telephone directory for the Virgin Islands reveals three subscribers surnamed Cuffy and one Quamina in St. Thomas; St. Croix has one Quamie. These processes escaped writers like Elsdon Smith, who were totally innocent of Creole studies and of background in the Herskovitsian tradition. Smith wrote:

> African names tended to remind them [freed slaves] of their former bondage, and were not used as family names (*American Surnames*, p. 275).

It apparently never occurred to Smith that a really independent-minded Black would find Cuffe less reminiscent of his former bondage than Slocum, the name of his former owner. Smith does provide some description of how other surnames were acquired by the Blacks and does go about as far as conventional wisdom will take us:

Employers [of Negro laborers in World War I] required full names. Conscripts in the army had to settle on a permanent surname which, upon marriage, became a hereditary family name. Social security laws were most effective in stabilizing the colored man's name (p. 276).

But the nickname (the name by which a person is actually called by his peers and parents) is largely beyond the control of owners, draft boards, and other such oppressive agencies. Furthermore, since plantation servants were often given charge of their masters' children, even those names applied to white children might show some influences from the practices of slaves. It is not true, although it has often been so maintained, that similarity (of naming practices or anything else) between Southern whites and Blacks is proof that the pattern originated with the whites. Nicknames are, obviously enough, the domain of onomastics which could be most completely controlled by the slaves – and, therefore, where retention of African patterns would be most likely. We find, furthermore, very widespread evidence like the occurrence, in Samaná, Dominican Republic, of the nickname Iso (from Umbundu or Yoruba, according to Turner 1949) for a man otherwise known as Walter among descendants of Black slaves who came from the Philadelphia area around 1840 (Hoetink 1962).

The existence of nicknames provides for a certain variability of onomastic practices – in Black or in any other context – and variability of Black former slaves has been observed in historical records – even by Elsdon Smith. Henderson H. Donald, in *The Negro Freedman* (1952) reported

For instance, a boy entered school under the name of Joseph Marshall; the boys called him Marshall Black; and the name given him by his parents, and by which he was called at home, was Joseph Black Thomas (p. 151).

Perhaps the most important recent theoretician of proper names (Algeo 1973: 56) has called attention to this 'arbitrariness characteristic of family names among the Black population of the South in the immediately postbellum years' and has asserted that they 'changed those names at will'. Algeo, who is not concerned with specifically Black matters, does not take up either the matter of nicknames or the use of day names for family names. His example, however, is just as clearly an example of a nickname as of a changing family name.

Among the name changers – and among the most conscious and militant of the Black opposers of white domination – of an early period was Sojourner Truth, a crusader not only for Black but also for feminine equality.[15] The story has been often told how she was known as the slave girl Isabela until about the age of twenty, when she was freed, left her master's plantation, and had a vision which told her of her mission and her new name. Etymologically, no one would take either *Sojourner* or *Truth* for an Africanism. But the narrowly etymological approach, which looks only at the origin of individual words,[16] has been the culprit here, causing us to miss very much what we would surely have seen if our vision had been broader. Perhaps, also, in the case of someone like Algeo a little more specifically African information would have helped to avoid some misemphases if not mistakes. Algeo wrote of the variability of the names of emancipated slaves:

> That arrangement, however, was clearly not normal, but rather a transitional one in which members of the population that had no family name system were acquiring one; in the process they treated 'family' names like given names, which need not be shared by members of the family unit, and both like nicknames, which can be freely changed at the whim of the name-users (1973: 57).

'Not normal and transitional' as it may be, the kind of name-shifting which Isabela indulged in has a great deal of West African precedent. Schneider (1965) reports that 'in many parts of West Africa, every man who leaves his traditional setting and family is given or takes on a new name when he travels or works away from home'. The vehicle of this name-shifting is Pidgin English, the most useful language for a West African worker when he moves into a polyglot environment where his tribal language will no longer suffice. To a degree, this situation parallels that of the slaves who were brought to the Americas, away from their own tribal ways and language but still in contact with Africans who shared some typological background.

Among the names listed by Schneider are[17]

I Go Try (I'll Try)
Banana Ret (Ripe Bananas)
Bad Belly
Botter Bia (Bottle of Beer)

God Love (God's Love, with
possession by juxtaposition)
Go 'Way
Good No De (Good Does Not

Chop Massa (Master of Eating – Gourmet)
Day di Go (Day is Passing)
Fine Boy
Free Boy
Gita Massa (Master of the Guitar – Guitarist)
God De (God Is, or Exists)
Exist)
Head Pan
Jam Pass Die (Poverty Worse Than Death)
Koni (Cunning) Boy
Long Boy
Long Long (Very Long)[18]
Lawyer

Schneider's list is much longer, and of course it does not exhaust the possibilities. Some of the factors in the choice of the names are obvious: Fine Boy hopes to become a houseboy (*steward*, in the English of the West Cameroon; *boy* in the French of the East Cameroun, where few seem to know that it is a loanword from English).

Although both Herskovits's and Schneider's investigations were made in recent times, historical sources confirm our feeling that this is no new development. In 1791, slave ship captain Hugh Crow wrote,

> We had on board a fine black boy, brought from Bonny, named 'Fine Bone'.[19]

Names of this type seem to have been in use about as long as the contact situation with the Europeans and the attendant use of Pidgin English (or Pidgin French, Pidgin Portuguese in different contact situations). What must have been true of the uprooted West Africans who fell victims to the Atlantic slave trade, who were wanted for laborers (and for almost nothing else), who entered into new cultural and linguistic relationships, and who (in spite of what some virtually ahistorical historians have thought) must have had to communicate with their fellows? Must such communication not have included calling others by name, and telling others their own names? And was it not as likely in the New World in the seventeenth, eighteenth, and nineteenth centuries as it is in the twentieth century in Africa that the tribal names of the native village would not serve in the new environment?

Herskovits, in his seminal work on African cultural survivals among Negroes in the United States, pointed out 'the ease with which a Negro may assume one name after another, especially in dealing with whites'.[20] Name-shifting is certainly attested in the records of slavery. Puckett's article lists, from the Esher Parish Register in Louisiana,

> Bacchus *alias* Hogtub *alias* Fat Jack, *alias* John.[21]

He also records a slave boy Malachi who 'was baptized seven times, under different names, and with different sponsors'.[22] Harriet Beecher Stowe's *The Key to Uncle Tom's Cabin* cites advertisements for runaway slaves from newspapers like the *Savannah Daily Georgian* (September 6, 1852) of a 'negro woman ... arrested ... under suspicious circumstances' who called herself Phebe, or Phillis. Elsewhere, the plantation literature quite regularly reports such acquired names – rather more representational in nature than has become the fashion in European naming practices – of its Black characters. We need not go so far as Stowe's Topsy Turvy (whose name obviously reflects how she 'just growed') to find examples. Frederick Law Olmsted, a severe critic of slavery and of Southern masters who nevertheless had the good sense to utilize what information he could get from them, was among many such reporters of the pattern. In *A Journey in the Back Country*, an overseer is represented as reporting

> That fellow ahead there, with the blue rag on his head, his name is Swamp; he always goes by that name, but his real name is Abraham, I believe (I: 91).

The name Swamp is an apparent contradiction of the pattern, since it is reported that the master gave it:

> He was bought of Judge ——, he says, and he told me his master called him Swamp because he ran away so much [that is, probably, into the swamps].

But it is notable that the actual transmission of the name to the current master was through the slave. Furthermore, the name fits the name-shifting pattern perfectly. What very likely happened was that the name-shifting was so prevalent that the Southern owners caught the spirit of it.

The pattern of nicknaming is very widespread in Afro-America. Dutch informants in Surinam told me that the Creoles frequently gave lasting nicknames because of a passing event or because of some action or feature of appearance. Examples were *Torpedohoofd* and Gimme Papa (from the latter's begging tendencies). An observer in the Bahamas and the West Indies writes that the prevalence of nicknames among men 'is truly striking', and lists names like 'Froggie', 'Cracker', 'Kingfisher', 'Peter Rabbit', 'Salt and Pepper', 'Brick Dust', 'Buggy Whip', 'Fleas', and many others.[23]

In the inner city in the United States, the nickname is equally important. On January 11, 1975, a fourteen-year-old Black boy named Charles Thomas was killed by a moving subway train in Brooklyn as he tried to spray-paint his nickname, 'Stim'. In the words of his grief-stricken mother 'The more trains they had their names on, the more important it made them feel'.[24] According to the *New York Times* (January 22, 1975, p. 17), Black mayor of Detroit Coleman A. Young, described as 'folksy, gregarious, and silverhaired', still 'hobnobbed with boyhood friends like Dirty Red and Skate Key'. All the focus on the inner city, as usual in such contexts, may tend to foster the pseudo-ecological interpretation that such nicknaming practices are in some strange way responses to the pressures of urban living. Stranger theories have been advanced: Some of the early investigators of Black language (Deutsch 1964) assumed that the slum environment was responsible for the development of Black English. Where names are concerned, we have a great deal of evidence that the 'urban' pattern was merely brought along with the Black population as they moved from rural areas. Among the many groups which illustrate this principle are the professional Black athletes. For example, William (the Bird) Averitt, guard for the Kentucky Colonels of the American Basketball Association, came from Kentucky's southwest badlands, where

> ... the kids were big on nicknames. They were not Billy, Steve, or Joe, they were 45, Eddieruff, Crow and Slim. It was there, on an improvised basketball court, that William Averitt, the Kentucky Colonels' backcourt man, picked up the name, the Bird (*New York Times*, January 25, 1975, p. 19).

In St. John, Virgin Islands, residents are often better known by their nicknames (e.g., Poodoo) than by their official names and will introduce themselves to strangers by those nicknames. Children in school sometimes carry over nicknames from their fathers. One father was known as Butcher because he had cut off some of his own fingers in an accident. The older son was also known as Butcher, and the younger as Baker. Another boy was called Gogo because of his ability to run fast.

In Puerto Rico, nicknames are of extreme importance in the Loiza-Carolina area, where the population is overwhelmingly Black. A boy known as Yuquita ('little yucca plant') or a man known as Nene ('Boy' or 'Buddy') may not be known even to fairly close acquaintances by any other name. Loiza Aldeans have told me that the mail delivery is often according to nickname and that a letter addressed by baptismal name may be delayed. Manning (1974) reports a parallel case from Barbados.

In New York City, Puerto Ricans who are often, like author Piri Thomas, dark-skinned or Black are in intimate culture contact with American Blacks. The nicknaming traditions reinforce each other in Spanish Harlem. Kohn and Hinton (1972: 120) have found that

> The names they chose for themselves were intentionally bizarre in the context of their society because they wanted to differentiate themselves from it. They laughed at [their teacher's] notion of 'legal' names because they considered the society illegal.

These children, whether Black American or Puerto Rican, scrawl nicknames like Bolita ('Little Ball') on the walls. They manifest name-shifting:

Bolita as Johnny Cool
Clarence as Lefty ∼ Lefty as Clarence
Alice as Slick ∼ Slick as Alice

Kohn and Hinton discuss in detail how these predominantly Puerto Rican children regard the names as a basic part of their own identity and tell how a teacher was assaulted in a Manhattan junior high school because he refused to address several of his pupils by the names which they considered their own. The upper and middle class often refuse to use these nicknames, or use them more sparingly than does the working class. In Jamaica, lower class names show important differences from the more assimilated and acculturated group. The former may be characteristically

Boy-Boy   Man-man
Evadney   Micey

where the first and third reflect a characteristically Afro-Creole reduplication pattern.[25] The latter group is more likely to be represented by conventional names like Andrew, Stephen, Philip, Carl, and Raymond. The obviously most important factor here is that the working class has had much less opportunity for assimilation to British and American ways than the middle or upper class.

Socio-economic factors are not, however, the only influential factor in the retention of the pattern of the use of nicknames. In the United States, one group which has had a certain amount of financial success, musicians and entertainers, has most notably retained this pattern. Everyone knows that jazzmen have had picturesque nicknames, like 'Jelly Roll', 'Satchmo', 'Yardbird', 'Lady', and 'Prez', or 'President'. Jazz *aficionados* know the stories of how these names derived from attributes of the musicians or from events in their lives. One of the oldest Black folk singers whose name is known was Old Corn Meal, who sold his product in New Orleans in the 1840's.[26] Not so many know how variable the names have been, so that Ferdinand La Menthe, who became Jelly Roll Morton, had earlier been known as Winding Ball or Winding Boy or Wining Boy,[27] or how the late blues singer Josh White was known as The Singing Christian and Pinewood Tom in earlier stages of his musical career.

In the case of Jelly Roll Morton, the pattern of changing names to adapt to new circumstances is transparently obvious. Ferdinand La Menthe, proud of his classical musical training as of his family's (like godmother Laura Hunter, a reputed voodoo witch also known as Eulalie Echo) appreciation for the recitals at the French opera house in New Orleans, wanted to play the piano but was sidetracked to the guitar temporarily because of a feeling that playing the piano left him open to suspicions about his masculinity. Returning to the piano, he took the first known nickname, Winding Ball (or Winding Boy), with its sexual connotations, as a kind of defense against the accusations of effeminacy and immaturity which might come to a very young player of the piano in the houses of prostitution in Storyville. After all, the best of the pianists of the tenderloin, Tony Jackson, was a known homosexual.[28] The manner in which he acquired the nickname Jelly Roll, during a comedy act in which the light-colored musician actually wore blackface, is one of the classics of jazz history:

Sandy [another comedian, in a kind of battle of jokes] said to me, 'You don't know who you're talking to.' ... He said he was Sweet Papa Cream Puff, right out of the bakery shop. That seemed to produce a great big laugh and I was standing there, mugging, and the thought came to me that I better say something about a bakery shop, so I said to him that he didn't know who *he* was talking to. He wanted to get acquainted, so I told him I was Sweet Papa Jelly

Roll with stove pipes in my hips and all the women in town just
dying to turn my damper down.[29]

The apparent improvisation of a new nickname involves, upon reflection, not so much innovation. The 'folk simile of sexual reference' fits
into the pattern of nicknames which La Menthe/Morton had chosen
before.[30] The aggregation which he assembled under the name of Jelly
Roll Morton and His Red Hot Peppers was the onomastic epitome of
the sex-*cum*-music connotations of the word *jazz*,[31] both in his own
name and in the connotations of *hot*.[32] It might be absurd to call the
name of the famous band an 'Africanism'; but is it not equally absurd
to overlook the obvious cultural continuity in the choosing of the
group's name? Black entertainers in other fields had the same predilection for nicknames.[33] Black comic dancers like Stringbeans and Sweetie
Mae and their followers Butterbeans and Susie were husband-and-wife
teams whose insult jokes suggested, at some remove, even Kingfish and
Sapphire of the Amos and Andy radio program.[34] The radio had blackface teams like Molasses and January and Sugar Cane and February;
but there were more genuine teams like Bilo and Asher, Son and Sonny,
Cook and Brown, Moke and Poke, Stump and Stumpy, Chuck and Chuck-
les, Red and Struggy, and a 'Two-story Tom', so called because of his
height, who picked up a partner in each town as he traveled the circuits.[35]
Virtually every writer who has dealt with the Black assumed names
or nicknames has commented on the exoticism involved. Puckett reported that of 5,034 female slaves in the records which he examined,
1,352 'had names which would be considered unusual according to
present-day white standards in the South; 1,018, however, had names
like Abigail, Deborah, and Saphronia, which would today be regarded
as merely old-fashioned'.[36] He was, however, somewhat under-inclined
to allow for the acculturation pressures or even outright white recorder
distortion of the official records. Nevertheless, he was to some degree
convinced by such names as Bituminous, Snowrilla, Vanilla, Precious
Pullins, Jeremiah Chronicles, and Magnolia Zenobia Pope.[37] Less
formal observers report names like Chamey (a woman), Queen Esther
Hawkins, and Dimple Dupree Hawkins (from Nacogdoches, Texas).
It is tempting to regard 'outlandish' names like these, which attract the
ready intuitive judgment by mainstream speakers as exotic or bizarre,
as evidence of African survivals at some remove, just as it is tempting
to regard Positive Wasserman Johnson – listed by Mencken – as an

example of the acquired nickname. They turn up in an overwhelming variety of contexts like the Western frontier, where 'Deadwood Dick' and '80 John' were only two of many. The overwhelming need, however, seems to be for an in-depth consideration of some natural corpus of such names. Because of the many studies (e.g., Jones 1963; Schuller 1968; Stearns 1956) which demonstrate definite non-Western elements in their music, jazzmen and blues musicians seem to constitute the best available such group. Both 'bizarreness' and the half-secret maintaining of ties with the 'hip' inner circle are probably involved in the nicknames of jazzmen from the beginning, as well as in the names which they gave to their bands (although both, especially the latter, are always suspect of commercial exploitation). From the beginning of jazz history,[38] we find names like Buddy or King Bolden, Bunk (born Willie) Johnson, Satchelmouth (Louis, also Satchmo) Armstrong, Kid Ory, King Oliver (Joe at birth, but also known as 'Bad Eye' to his intimates for some time – supposedly because street urchins in New Orleans took notice of a boomstick wound which contracted his eyebrows into a puzzled scowl),[39] Big Eye Louis,[40] 'Ratty' John Vean, 'Zino' (Henry Baltimore, a drummer), and very many others.

Any list would have to be incomplete – and suspect for bias. My own inclination, for example, had been to leave off Cow Cow Davenport because his nickname so obviously derives from song lyrics – until I learned that the lyrics in question had been written by his wife, who also worked as a snake charmer.[41] 'Fats', for Thomas Waller, may have been primarily for commercial purposes – but so, too, was The Red Hot Peppers. It could hardly be considered that the assigning of a nickname carried no traces of a cultural pattern simply because the nickname was used for commercial purposes. More or less prosaic explanations might come from a closer study of the biography of anyone on the list, but 'exotic' overtones (by middle-class American standards) are not likely to be eliminated completely. With that expression of diffidence, then, the list:

Cripple Clarence Lofton	Jabbo Smith
Sugar Johnny	Little Junior Parker
Blind Blake	Little Richard
Blind Willie Matell	Stormy Williams
Theodore 'Doc' Ross	'Papa' Charlie Jackson
Leo 'Snub' Moseley	Big Maceo Merriwether

Speckled Red
Charlie 'Big' Green
Aaron 'T-Bone' Walker
Willis 'Gatortail' Jackson
Dink Johnson
Pine Top
Frankie 'Half Pint' Jaxon
Mule Bradford
Champion Jack Dupre
Leonard 'Lucky' Enois
LeRoy 'Snake' White
Clarence 'Frog' Anderson
Blind Lemon Jefferson
'Cootie' Williams
Henry 'Kid' Rena
Black Pete
Geechy Fields
Billy Holliday 'Lady Day'
'Little Goat'
Willie 'the Lion' Smith
Memphis Slim
Eddie 'Cleanhead' Vinson
Bumble Bee Slim
Joe 'Tricky Sam' Nanton
Mutt Carey
Pop Foster
Big Bill Broonzy

Sonny Boy Williams
Fats Domino
Bull City Red
Boogie Woogie Red
Blind Boy Fuller
Little Junior Parker
Count Basie
Duke Ellington
Sir Charles Thompson
Tubby Hale
Hot Lips Page
Zutty Singleton
Julian 'Cannonball' Adderly
King Curtis
Earl 'Fatha' Hines
Scrapper Blackwell
Tampa Red
'Bull Moose' Jackson
Chubby Checker
'Blind' Gary Davis
Blind Willie Johnson
Lil Son Jackson
Lark Lee
Soap Stick
Long Boy
Barrel House Tom
Orville 'Piggie' Minor

Temporary, improvised, and shifting names have been very much part of the jazz scene. Mezzrow tells of Tommy Ladnier's forming an up-town club called the Fish Club, in which Ladnier was the King Fish, Mezzrow was Father Neptune, and Sidney Bechet was The Flounder. Nothing, however, is equal to the array of names which Harlem street-corner society applied to Mezzrow himself. The Reefer King, The Link Between The Races, The Philosopher, The Mezz, Poppa Mezz, Mother Mezz, Pop's Boy, The White Mayor of Harlem, The Man About Town, The Man That Hipped The World, The Man That Made History, The Man With The Righteous Bush, He Who Diggeth The Digger, Father Neptune.

When we compare white jazzmen's names, the quantitative difference in the traditions becomes obvious, even if it not be allowed that there is an essential content difference:

Pee Wee Russell	Muggsy Spanier
Milton 'Mezz' Mezzrow	Husk O'Hara
Jess Stacey	Dick MacPartland
Frank 'Tesch' Teschmaier	Joseph 'Sharkey' Bonano
'Wild Bill' Davison	Eddie Condon
Willy Guitar	Emile 'Stale Bread' Lacoume, Sr.
Jack Teagarten	Emile 'Whiskey' Benrod
Bix Beiderbecke	Albert 'Slew-foot Pete' Montluzin
Benny Goodman	Cleve 'Warm Gravy' Craven

The only ones of these nicknames which seem even roughly comparable are the last few,[42] where there is a heavy Cajun influence. This is in spite of the fact that there was a reverse acculturative influence in jazz: Whites often tried to become as much like Negroes as possible. Mezz Mezzrow, whose *Really the Blues* contains probably the most overt of such statements, has a nickname which is astonishingly prosaic and 'secular' – being, of course, just a short form of his surname – for one so eager to adapt himself to the Black tradition.

There is a further suggestion in the names which Caribbean Calypsonians choose for themselves. The best known of these is, of course, The Mighty Sparrow. Others, like the not so well known Mighty Spitfire who was playing around the bars in Trinidad in 1965, have obviously conformed to the same pattern. Lord Burgess, Lord Melody, Lord Rhaburn (from British Honduras), Lord Invader, Lord Superior, Lord Shortie, Lord Kitchener, King Pharoah, and King Radio are of another pattern, recalling to some degree the King, Duke, and Count of American jazzmen. In the Virgin Islands in January, 1975, posters proclaimed that King Obstinate (a former Antiguan calypso singer now a night club owner) was presenting The Mighty Swallow in concert. Others told, in December of 1974, of the coming of Mighty Duke, four times calypso king of Trinidad, and Princess Shirlana Strip Tease Belly Dancer. Other calypsonians include The Duke of Iron, Attila the Hun (*alias* Shakespeare), The Might Chalkdust ('Chalkie'), Lord Eisenhower, King Richard the Lion Heart (or Richard Coeur-de-Lion), Small Island Pride, Dapet Tie Pin, Lord Inventor, Gorilla, Mighty Bird, Lord Short Shirt, Tiger, Calypso Rose, Singing Francine, and the Mighty

Swallow. A limbo dancer is known as Prince Rupert. In Jamaica, singer Pluto Shervington is advertised as the Ram Goat Liver Man (*Kingston Daily Gleaner*, Nov. 14, 1974, p. 5).

Taking into consideration the West Indian parallels, it seems very unlikely that the Black personal names, especially the names of jazz and blues musicians and entertainers, can be taken merely as reflections of European patterns. In fact, it has been frequently suggested that Black patterns had more influence on white culture in certain, primarily less formal, domains than has been generally accepted. As keepers of white children in their most formative years, Negro 'mammies' and their children on the plantation had a fine – but generally unrecognized – opportunity to impose their patterns on the formally dominant group.[43] B. Carridine wrote of the onomastic influence:

> . . . few such appelations [of Southern white parents to their children] escaped a beheading, reheading and often entire change at the hands of the family servants. One of the prerogatives assumed and tacitly granted the slave in the South was this accolade touch and bedub-bing process by which a nickname was given a child instead of his own. . . . An additional fact of surprise was that the parents them-selves at least fell into the use of the terms given by the Negro sponsors, and the beautiful, elegant cognomens of Edwin, Gerald, Blanche, and Grace would utterly disappear, and the strange, gro-tesque applications of 'Ripper', 'Snorter', 'Coon', 'Possum', 'Boots', 'Horse', 'Dan Tucker', and many others like them would remain victors in the field.[44]

2. Jazz, Blues, and Rock Bands and Their Titles

If Ferdinand LaMenthe/Morton's nickname 'Jelly Roll' fits into an essentially Black tradition, and if the name of his finest band, the Red Hot Peppers, shares the sexual allusions of his own nickname as well as seeming otherwise consistent with the same tradition, then the important question of the provenience of the band names seems automatically to be raised. The Red Hot Peppers were not, of course, the only group which Morton directed. (The term 'fronted', which is perhaps appropriate to some bandleaders, was completely inapplicable to Ferd/Jelly Roll.) His last session, arranged for by Hughes Panassie the French jazz critic, was with a unit called Jelly Roll Morton and His New Orleans Jazzmen; and there were other such units (probably not all of them ever identified by name) along the way. But the makeup of bands in the American popular tradition is an extremely impermanent matter, and names tend to change about as rapidly as personnel reorganizations are made. Any kind of claim about specifically Black naming patterns for the bands will have to be based on some other kind of evidence.

As often in the materials under examination in this book, the scanty early records provide no obvious and direct link to Africa. The earliest brass bands, generally recognized as the most direct forerunners of the jazz bands,[1] tended to be known by the names of the plantations where the men continued to work.[2] Other groups chose names, often quite ordinary ones, from places like Laneville and Bogue Chitto. (Any 'bizarreness' in the latter would of course come from the place name itself.) Two of the groups might join forces to produce, for example, the Laneville-Johnson Union Brass Band.[3] Worshippers from different congregations also formed bands to play hymns and took names from the places of origin.

By the time Bunk Johnson was playing in bands for funerals, Labor Day, carnival, and Club 'prades' [parades] and other such activities in New Orleans, there were brass bands with names like

The Old Teao
Charlie Dablayes Brass Band
The Diamond Stone Brass Band
The Old Excelsior Brass Band
The Algiers and Pacific Brass Band
Kid Allen's Father Brass Band
Frank Duson Eagle Brass Band
George McCullons Brass Band
Silver Bell Band[4]

If the name could be adequately supported philologically, *Kid Allen's Father Brass Band* would show the Black English grammatical feature of possession by juxtaposition ('unmarked' possessive); but names in general are not very good sources for grammatical structures. One or two of the names begin to show a bit of exoticism; but Johnson also specified that he played with many 'no names brass bands' – apparently ones that could not afford the luxury of a name or did not bother with one.[5]

For the person thoroughly familiar with the geography and life of New Orleans in the early twentieth century, some of the exocitism might of course be dispelled. *Algiers* in the first name above refers not to the African country but to a town across the river from New Orleans, home of (among others) the great trumpeter Henry (Red) Allen. My informants[6] have not been able to identify the component *Pacific* for me, except to suggest that perhaps it referred to the Texas and Pacific Railroad, which passed through New Orleans. The combination – if indeed that is the correct explanation – is idiosyncratic by mainstream American standards, at any rate.

Some elements of bizarreness or exoticism disappear, then, in the glare of mundane details; but further examination reveals replacements. Glittering names for the bands did not die out with the old brass bands, but rather burst forth in special new splendor with what are usually considered the first jazz bands proper in New Orleans. There were such later groups as

Kid Ory's Brown Skinned Jazz Band

The Red Onion Jazz Babies
The Original Creole Band
The Onward Band
The Halfway House Gang
The New Orleans Rhythm Kings
(Freddy Keppard's) Tuxedo Band

And of course there was the first white imitation – in more ways than one – the Original Dixieland Jazz Band. Ignoring precise chronology, we can cite other relatively early Black groups:

Louis Armstrong and His Stompers
Louis Armstrong's Hot Five
Clarence Williams' Blue Five
Dave Peyton's Symphonic Syncopators
Fate Marable's Jazz-E-Sazz Band
Southern Syncopated Orchestra
The Musical Spillers
Johnny Dodds's Washboard Band
Johnny Dodds's Black Bottom Stompers

One of the most important early groups was billed as 'Kid Ory's Seven Pods of Pepper, with Ory's Creole trombone' and also as 'Ory's Brown Skinned Band'. The word *pepper*, as in Morton's band, obviously carried on the associations of *hot*, which are quite important for Afro-American music.

White imitators ranged from Mezz Mezzrow and His Percolatin' Fools, led by a musician who profusely acknowledged and even flaunted his debt to the Negroes, to Bob Crosby and His Bobcats, whose leader apparently never expressed himself on the subject. Except for Mezzrow's bands, white groups had names which are extremely tame by Black standards, even when we consider potential commercial exploitations like that of comedian-to-be Jimmy Durante and his Jazz and Novelty Band.

Mezzrow, who was almost aggressively Black in culture and who must have been one of the first to proclaim the superiority of Black patterns over white, tells, in *Really the Blues*, how he overheard the use of the term *perculate* by a Black speaker (referring to a band's performance, in something of the same sense that *swing it!* later came to have), was struck by its appropriateness, and consciously incorporated it into the name of his first band. Some of his later organizations, which were just as consciously Black-oriented, were Mezz Mezzrow and His Purple Grackle Orchestra, Mezz Mezzrow and His Swing Band, and Mezz Mezzrow and His Disciples of Swing.[8]

The most significant Black band names of them all, however, may have been formulated at an earlier date. They were applied to Army bands in Europe during World War I, and had little attention commercially. Two of these, appropriately part of the U.S. Expeditionary Force in Europe, were headed by a musician named James Europe: Three Hundred and Sixty-Ninth U.S. Infantry Hell-Fighters Band, and the Clef Club Orchestra. Others were called the Fifty Joy Whooping Sultans of High Speed Syncopation, the Fifty Merry Moguls of Melody, and the Forty Black Devils. In the segregated army of that period, they were all-Black units – an unfortunate social fact, but a strange left-handed boon for the onomastician, since there can be little doubt of the Black provenience of the names under those conditions.

Apparently, little was made of these 'bizarre' or 'exotic' names, although the American (and, to some degree, the European) public must have been aware of them. Except for a few culture-shifters like Mezz Mezzrow, however, there was little influence on the white world, unless we regard Paul Whiteman's designation as the 'King of Jazz' and Benny Goodman's as 'King of Swing' as trite (and rather bogus) applications of a naming tradition that began with King Bolden and King Oliver and involved the yearly naming of a King of the Zulus among the Black participants in Mardi Gras.

In the nineteen-sixties, however, the copying of Black styles by certain white bands became both a rallying point for youth and a big business.[9] These groups, copying the 'race' musicians whose work came to have the designation 'rock and roll', imitated the 'freaky' song titles and lyrics and band names which rock and roll shared with jazz.[10] The designation *rock and roll* may owe something, as terminology, to *rock and reel*, religious songs in the Black churches that 'truly shake the rafters'.[11] The musically fastidious have often complained that neither Black nor white practitioners of the genre were up to the artistic level of the best blues- and jazzmen,[12] but rock and roll was a much greater commercial success than either of its predecessors. Besides, who really believes that the most typical representatives of a culture are its greatest artists?

As it hit the American teenager and his often-suffering elders, rock and roll was propagated by a group of British boys who wore their hair long, cultivated at least the terminology of drugs and other bizarre activities, and borrowed from American Negro musical styles – although perhaps at second hand.[13] They were not the first but they were commercially the most successful of a series of gaudily named groups which came to include Gerry and the Pacemakers, The Swinging Blue Jeans, The Merseybeats, The Hollies, The Kings, The Byrds, The Lovin' Spoonful, The Mamas and Papas, and The Beach Boys. If they did not launch they at least popularized the trend from which it seems that American popular music will never recover. In their early attempts to attract attention, they called themselves Johnny and the Moondogs, the first element obviously representing John Lennon, their leader, and the second perhaps influenced by an old Negro musician who had played around the streets of Manhattan and had been fairly well known to the show business crowd and the Broadway columns – Moondog.[14] The aggregation (which grew out of a group which John Lennon first of all called the Quarrymen) shifted its name with rather obvious publicity-seeking intent, becoming first The Silver Beatles and then just The Beatles. The final name, especially, linked them to self-conscious imitation of Black life styles – the Beat or Beatnik movement, the most revealing work in which may have been Norman Mailer's *The White Negro*. A great deal has been written about the artistic merits of this movement – and a great deal more has been thought and uttered between clenched teeth, particularly where the musical combos are concerned.[15] This is no place for such considerations.

At any rate, it may be that another British group, which made its impact much later, was more directly responsible for inculcating Black values into white rock and roll. According to John M. Hellman, Jr.,[16] The Rolling Stones were the group which

> ... 'dropped out' in the early 60's to spend their time playing a decidedly ungenteel American Negro music known as rhythm and blues and went on to become the primary artistic figures in a mass transfusion of American urban Negro attitudes into the dominant white cultures of both America and Britain.[17]

The Black 'argot' which Hellman found the Rolling Stones picking up is that manifestation of Black English, considered superficial by the linguist,[18] known as ethnic slang. It is interesting that Hellman notes the use of *jelly roll* ('either for the vagina or for the sexual act itself because of its sweetness and its rhythmic design') both by Black blues musicians and by the Rolling Stones. He also points out the use, by Mick Jagger and his group, of 'traditional [phrases] of the old blues' like 'kick in the stall', 'lemon squeeze' (citing a famous use by Bessie Smith), 'monkey man', 'rider', 'cherry red', and 'toys'; these, he says, 'create lyrics that use a unique but subtle variation of the blues argot'.[19]

If The Beatles and The Rolling Stones are relatively conventional names, other rock and roll bands – as everyone who is not blessed with a residence in an ivory tower must now know – have fancy, extraordinary names. They are called Big Brother and the Holding Company, Sly and the Family Stone, Led Zeppelin, The Grateful Dead, Fifth Dimension, Humble Pie, and other such names.[20] A list, which would probably not impress the veriest pre-teen neophyte by its completeness, follows:

Three Dog Night	Ten Years After
Bachman-Turner Overdrive	Iron Butterfly
Steppenwolf	Steely Dan
Grand Funk	Stealer's Wheel
Rare Earth	Bee Gees
Guess Who	Deep Purple
Black Sabbath	Faces
Carpenters	The Electric Prune
Bread	Band of Gypsies
The Animals	The Mamas and the Papas
Mothers of Invention	Traffic
The Yardbirds	Bad Company
The Who	Yes
Cream	The Monkees
The Incredible String Band	Kozmic Blues Band
Pink Floyd	Fugs
Cactus	Full Tilt Boogie Band
Country Joe and the Fish	

There are also prominent rocksters like Alice Cooper, whose name seems far from bizarre until one realizes that it belongs to a non-transvestite male singer, and that he publicizes himself by a pretense of sadism. In these names, Steppenwolf seems an unusual reference to German romantic novels; but we must remember that Johnny Dodds did a blues version of the tenor aria from *I Pagliacci* under the name of

'Blue Washboard Stomp', and that Jelly Roll Morton was proud of his adaptations from the romantic opera. (That was what he meant, most of the time, when he boasted of his 'classical music' background.) Grand Funk has an obvious reference to the vocabulary of the ghetto,[21] and at least some informants have been willing to accept my interpretation that the Mothers of Invention represent a variation (now somewhat more obscene in the Black community than the word for which it originally was a euphemism) on The Motherfuckers of Invention. The voodoo elements which Jelly Roll Morton kept well hidden from the public are obviously not represented in the white rock tradition, but Black Sabbath does to some degree represent the seeking for exotic religious elements which sent the Beatles on their famed and well-publicized pilgrimages to the Guru of India.

The list of 'far out' elements on the rock scene could hardly be complete without mention of song titles. Perhaps typical is Jimi Hendrix's 'Have You Ever Been to Electric Ladyland?' There is a certain amount of continuity with Hendrix's other activities in the title, since Electric Ladyland was the recording studio in which he reportedly tried to 'do his own thing' – away from the stereotyped activities which he felt had been imposed upon him by commercial managers. Hendrix has further titles like 'Third Stone from the Sun', 'And the Gods Made Love', 'Voodoo Child', 'Little Miss Strange', 'Burning of the Midnight Lamp', and 'All Along the Watchtower'. Humble Pie features songs like '30 Days in the Hole', 'Round Runners "G" Jam', and 'Sweet Peace and Time'. Cactus gives us 'Bad Mother[fucker?] Boogie',[22] 'Bedroom Mazurka', and 'Bad Stuff'. The Led Zeppelin group has many like 'Gallows Poll', 'Hats Off to Croys Harper', 'Brony-Aur-Stomp'. Rock poet Bob Dylan offers 'Subterranean Homesick Blues', 'Positively 4th Street', and a book entitled *Tarantula*.

Although not so self-consciously extreme, Jelly Roll Morton's own song titles are not exactly of the 'Night and Day', 'Stormy Weather', and 'Stardust' type. Many have remarked, like Charles Edward Smith, on how Jelly's titles often had 'an amusing Creole flavor'.[23] The sides he recorded included 'Frog-i-More Rag', 'Seattle Hunch', 'Burnin' the Iceberg', 'Futuristic Blues', 'Keep Your Business', 'New Crawley Blues', 'You Done Played Out', 'Crazy Chords', 'Low Gravy', 'Strokin' Away', 'Blue Blood Blues', 'Mushmouth Shuffle', 'Fickle Fay Creep', 'Sidewalk Blues', 'Dead Man Blues', 'Deep Creek', 'The Chant', 'Smokehouse Blues', and 'Grandpa's Spells'. The title 'Mr. Jelly Lord' requires special grammatical interpretation; it does not parse unless we imagine how it is performed:

Mr. Jelly – Lord! – he's really royal at the old keyboard.

'King Porter Stomp' sounds innocuous enough until we hear Jelly himself tell how the stomp was originally dedicated to a friend named Porter King.[24]

The titles of the blues corpus are, in fact, full of such bizarre matters, especially for one who is not inside the blues culture. 'Mojo Hand' would seem like a title in a foreign language to one who did not know of magic practices originally associated with voodoo and root magic.[25] Brief samplings of rural blues titles[26] produces 'Thousand Woman Blues' (Blind Boy Fuller), 'Milk Cow Blues' (Kokomo Arnold), 'Skin Game Blues' (Peg Leg Howell), 'From Four Till Late' (Robert Johnson). The great Sam 'Lightnin'' Hopkins, whom Charters once called 'the last of the bluesmen', has titles like 'Happy Blues for John Glenn', 'The Devil Jumped the Black Men', 'Black Cadillac', 'How Many More Years I Got to Let You Dog Me Around', 'Have to Let You Go', 'Down Baby', 'Fast Mail Rambler', and 'Sis' Boogie'. Jealous James Stanchell, on *A Treasury of Field Recordings*,[27] has 'Anything from a Foot Race to a Resting Place', and Lightnin' Hopkins and Jack Jackson have 'The Slop' on the same disk. No inventory could be complete without 'The Shit Out of Luck Blues', which the timid make into 'The S.O.L. Blues' and the Bowdlerizers into 'The Sure Out of Luck Blues'.

Like the Rural Blues, Country Blues[28] can seem simple and homey. The titles and the lyrics are, however, not simple: 'Key to the Highway' (Big Bill Broonzy), 'You Gonna Need Somebody on Your Bond' (Blind Willie Johnson), 'Low Down Rounder's Blues' (Peg Leg Howell). As far as that goes, Bessie Smith's 'Make Me a Pallet on the Floor' and 'Empty Bed Blues' are hardly the type of title played by Guy Lombardo.

The Beatles – like the Rolling Stones – were known for the scarcely hidden drug messages in their titles and in their lyrics: 'Yellow Submarine' ('downer' pills), 'Lucy in the Sky with Diamonds' (LSD), etc. Other groups features titles like 'Eat a Peach' (mushroom); Neil Young's 'I've Seen the Needle and the Damage Done'; Traffic's 'Light Up or Leave Me Alone'; Steppenwolf's 'The Pusher' and 'Magic Carpet Pride'; Hendrix's 'Are You Experienced?' and 'Purple Haze'; Bob Dylan's 'Rainy Day Women' ('They'll stone you . . . Everybody got to get stoned'), Arlo Guthrie's line 'Don't touch my bags, Mr. Customs

Man'. These were the (barely) hidden messages of the counter-culture, and again they had their Black forerunners. The unique study by Miles Mark Fisher (1953) shows how phrases like *promised land* in the Negro 'spirituals', now generally taken to refer to religious matters in the Judaeo-Christian tradition, actually were a means of transmitting messages about revolt, possible freedom, and even return to Africa. 'Zion', 'Paradise', and 'New Jerusalem' had the same kind of double significance, as did 'Jacob's Ladder'. Many other such examples can be found in Fisher's fascinating study. The transmitting of messages coded to confuse the master (or parent) is certainly a common factor in the pre-jazz music of the Negro as it is in the strange post-jazz world of rock music, listeners to which seem to give their allegiance more to drugs than to any class, ethnic, or political group.

But the expression of pro-drug sentiments in song titles was not new with the Beatles or the Rolling Stones, or any other such aggregation. Stuff Smith, whose very nickname refers to drugs, wrote 'If You're a Viper' around 1929, with very clear allusions to the activities of a *viper* ('marihuana smoker').[29] There were also 'If You'se a Viper', by Rosetta Howard; 'Sendin' the Vipers', by Mezz Mezzrow, and 'Viper's Drag', by Fats Waller. As Mezzrow's *Really the Blues* also shows, 'viper' allusions were common in vaudeville acts at the Lafayette Theatre in Harlem over forty years. Many who hear Bessie Smith sing 'Gimme a Pigfoot' on her famous record think she is singing about pork; but those who know that *pigfoot* means marihuana have a different kind of understanding. There are, in fact, many more such hidden allusions in the titles of jazz numbers.

In the far-out, 'freaky' names and song titles which they chose, in the conveying of messages in a covert manner, and to some extent in their direct use of Black ghetto 'argot', white rock bands have obviously been influenced by earlier practices of Black groups. It may be going too far to say that such influence amounted to direct imitation. However, it seems very unlikely that even the onomastics of popular music in the United States could have been the same if the Black jazz and blues tradition had not been around.

3. Church Names

Given the close relationship between various apparently secular Black music types and the church,[1] it would not be surprising that something of the same kind of unorthodox naming tradition could be found in religious institutions and related societies. In fact, what may be the clearest set of African-derived naming patterns seems to be in existence in the churches.

Even though the religiousness and devotion to the church of the Black community in the United States have been often proclaimed, the full impact of the non-secular element in Afro-American culture may not be recognized until one considers the religious and quasi-religious nature of many other kinds of societies. The tendency has often been noted for various American Blacks to belong to a Christian church while still engaging in the practice of magic or spiritualism which is vodun-tinged.[2] Jones (1963) makes it very explicit:

> But is was not unusual for a Negro to belong to the Christian church (in New Orleans, after the Black Codes of 1724, Negroes were only allowed to become Catholics) and to also belong to a number of secret societies. These societies still thrive all over the country in most Negro communities, although for the most part their actual 'secrecy' is the secrecy of any fraternal organization. The Masons and the Elks have claimed most urban and Northern Negroes, and the vodun-tinged secret orders, sometimes banned by whites, have for the most part (except in the rural areas) disappeared.[3]

In addition, some of these societies have obviously changed in the direction of being more churchlike. An obvious example is the Universal Christian International Catholic Church (Brooklyn, New York), presided over by His Holiness M. Zidoneo Hamatheite, Presiding Archepatriarche [sic] No. 1. The letterhead of the organization lists the names of other officials:

Elder B. R. E. Jebucitwa, Intl. Exec. Sec'y-Tres. Evan. Rakalmocina C. Hamatheite, Diocesan Sec'y. Deaconess E. Avista Cinita, Drive Booster

and the foreign representatives:

Princess Barcubuc Mamatheite, Field Sec'y. Princess Dedanelia Hamatheite, Field Booster. Prince James Hamatheite, Field Booster

In addition to the somewhat synthetic Ethiopianism[4] (long practiced by the militant Black community, with an effectiveness that need not concern us here), there are other cultural trends which seem glaringly obvious in this organization. One of them is the Black secret society and lodge tradition, with which any student of Black culture must have some familiarity. The other is the Protestant evangelical tradition, perhaps best associated with the Southern Black, as reflected in words like *Booster*. Its name proclaims the main activity of the group to be religious, but the letter I received from the Archepatriarche (soon after the publication of my *Black English*, and directly related thereto) asserted that the 'above named church is currently engaged in research in an effort to write a New African Language, based on the general syntax of the more than 800 languages which are now being spoken by various African ethnic groups in Africa'. The insignia on the letterhead also accords more nearly with lodges and secret societies than with a church group in the middle class white sense.

Lodge names among American Negroes are a familiar phenomenon, and many of them exhibit 'exotic' characteristics. These organizations have been very well documented for New Orleans, at least. Jelly Roll Morton remarked

New Orleans was very organization-minded. I have never seen such beautiful clubs as they had there – the Broadway Swells, the High Arts, the Orleans Aides, the Bulls and Bears, the Tramps, The Iroquois, the Allegroes – that was just a few of them.[5]

Another source reports

There are literally hundreds of Negro lodges, burial societies, and similar organizations in New Orleans. The following are only a few of the better known organizations:

Ladies Independence B.M.A.A.
Juvenile Cooperators Fraternal Society
Ladies Morality B.M.A.A.
Harmony B.M.A.A.
Young Friends of the B.M.A.A.
The New Ladies, Friends of Louisiana
Hall of the Ladies, Friends of Louisiana
Young Men's Provident B.M.A.A.
Ladies and Young Ladies St. Celena B.M.A.A.
Partisan's B.M.A.A.
Young Men of St. Michael B.M.A.A.
Ladies Kind Deeds B.M.A.A.
Ladies Protective B.M.A.A.
Young Friends of Order B.M.A.A.[6]

Many of them had names in French:
Société de Bienfaisance Mutuelle
Les Jeunes Amis
Société des Francs Amis
Nouvelle Société des Amis
Société des Amis Inséparables

Herskovits has pointed out that Dahomeyan society has many 'non-relationship groupings which resemble these lodges'.[8] Herskovits did not say anything about the names of the lodges and societies, either in the U.S. or in Dahomey. Silence, however, should not be interpreted to be equivalent of denial. Métraux, a persistent student of Africanisms in Haiti, devotes a rather long article[9] to Haitian work societies, claiming African survivals, but lets only one name slip in, almost as if by accident. The name is La Flè Kômas 'The Flower Is Commencing' Society.[10] The importance of these societies has frequently been recognized by students in the field. Samuel S. C. Adams pointed out

The fact that more plantation families belong to the burial associations than to the church may be regarded as significant.[11]

It is also very likely, of course, that these work societies and burial associations became somewhat less plentiful as the Black population moved into the Northern cities, although we have nothing approaching statistics. In the South Carolina and Georgia Low Country, a kind of beginning point for the whole process in some ways (Turner 1949; Wood 1975), mutual aid societies had names like Knights of Wise and Sisters of Zion.[12] There were also, in the area often also referred to as the Sea Islands, 'other local clubs or societies such as the Mutual Friendly Aid, the Jolly Boys, the Golden Link, the Seaside Branch, and the Union Gospel Traveller'.[13] On Chicago's South Side, there have been many organizations like The Sons and Daughters of I Do Arise. Mezzrow (*Really the Blues*) compared that one to the Knights of Pythias and the Elks. If societies of this type did indeed decrease in number as the Black population became more urban, many of their social functions – and even something of their naming pattern – were absorbed by the storefront church.

In recent years, students have increasingly noted the special characteristics of storefront church names in the Northern ghettoes, as well as in the South. In 1960, Thomas Fairclough perceived that

> The difference between white and Negro Baptists in New Orleans – between their attitudes toward the religion they practice and the world they live in – are probably mirrored quite accurately in the striking divergence of their church-naming patterns.[14]

Descriptions of religious differences by Mitchell (1972), Lomax (1959), and especially by Herskovits[15] have established the influence of syncretic survivals from West African religious practices in the American Black community. These are, of course, not limited to New Orleans, the South, or any particular geographic area. Neither are the naming practices, as Fairclough himself established when he compared two Black communities in Midwest cities – Lincoln, Nebraska, and Waterloo, Iowa:

> These cities have far fewer Baptist churches than New Orleans (eight in Lincoln, seven in Waterloo); but both provide confirmation, on a smaller scale, of the basic trend noted in the Southern city: whites favoring secular names, Negroes preferring religious.[16]

Just what Fairclough meant by *secular* and *religious* may be quite important; in fact, it may be the key to the entire problem of white and Black naming differences, something like *religious* even possibly replacing what has been called *exotic* or *bizarre* to this point.[17] Fairclough makes the point – which is very well taken, insofar as it goes – that whites take their church names from 'this present world', and particularly from their own immediate neighborhoods:

This would seem to indicate a primary concern for what religion can do in this world and for its people, rather than with the best way to prepare men for another world.[18]

Blacks, on the other hand, form their church names around

. . . some religious element, although by no means all are strictly religious, and several have no direct biblical derivation. The great popularity of definitely religious words and phrases in church names indicates that the religious life of the New Orleans Negro is otherworldly in its orientation, directed toward a consideration of a better life which is not here but to come.[19]

There is no doubt that the evidence of names elsewhere (see below for examples) matches that of the New Orleans Black churches.

The interesting question, however, is one that Fairclough does not deal with at all: Does 'otherwordly' refer to Heaven, or to Africa? If one assumes, as it is easy to do, that Black Christianity is and always has been an offshoot of white and European religion, then it is almost essential to conclude that 'otherworldly' refers to the concept of an afterlife. If, however, we look at a work like Miles Mark Fisher's *Negro Slave Songs in the United States* (1953) – in many respects the most important single book on the Negro in the United States – we see a strong suggestion that the 'other world' may be Africa. Fisher's materials (especially Chapters 3 and 4) show how the terminology of 'Negro spirituals' disguised the workings of an African cult which met to plan for return to Africa and even to plot the overthrow and death of the white masters. 'Steal Away', today a hymn almost universally taken literally(!) in its 'Steal away to Jesus' theme, was in the early nineteenth century a message convening a secret meeting. Fisher even traces authorship of that particular spiritual – with at least some credibility – to the famous revolutionary Nat Turner. Many others expressed their longings for freedom and return to their own land in songs the words of which could be interpreted to mean dedication to the otherworldliness of conventional religion. After the failure of Nat Turner's rebellion, according to Fisher, a great feeling of resignation set in, and many Negro Christians actually came to have the otherworldly feelings which the letter of the spirituals called for – ignoring, that is, the secret and more symbolic meanings. Fisher, like many others who are interested in 'messages' and not in structures, paid no attention to such matters as names of churches. It may well be, furthermore, that the elaborate names which Fairclough and others have noted did not exist in the period before Nat Turner's rebellion. But there are enough modern African parallels to the church naming patterns to make some connection apparent.

The names of West African churches, particularly those that are close to the African folk and have little European influence, are anything but secular. Geoffrey Parrinder (*Religion in an African City*, 1953) lists the following from Ibadan, names of what he calls 'Separatist Churches':

Sacred Cherubim and Seraphim Society (3)
New Eden Cherubim and Seraphim Church
St. Hagai's Cherubim and Seraphim Church
Holy Flock of Christ
The Apostolic Faith
Holy Ethiopian Community Church[20]
Ethiopian Communion Church
United Native African Church
Ebenezer African Church (Incorporated)
United African Methodist Church
Christ Apostolic Church
Christ Apostolic Gospel Church
Saviour Apostolic Church[21]

Onomastic parallels between the Nigerian Separatist churches and Black American storefront churches are striking; in fact, Parrinder details direct influence like the renunciation of infant baptism because of the influence of the Faith Tabernacle of Pennsylvania and the name of The Apostolic Faith 'of American inspiration, from the sect of this name in Portland, Oregon' (p. 126). Like Black American church names, however, those of the Nigerian Separatist churches seem to have a spontaneous and innovative quality. In an even more objective parallel, they often come about as the result of a kind of splinter movement; Parrinder tells how the majority of a Faith Tabernacle group "split away, and took the title of 'Christ Apostolic Church'. They are still often called 'Faith Tabernacle' or 'Precious Stone' (okuta iyebiye)" (p. 115).

Spontaneity may be less striking than conformity to an outsider, but the church members themselves give typical reports stressing the new creation of names. Parrinder tells how a splinter group will set up 'in a new part of town, as a result of a dream or vision in which some new name is revealed. Such churches are New Eden and Saint Hagai. The latter saint cannot be traced in the Bible or the hagiology, but the name was given in a vision'. A social psychology of dreaming might well stress the conformity to a pattern of such namings, but the people who are involved in the process obviously think of the names as the results of divine revelation and look upon them as completely new and original.

More like the Black American lodge officials than like those of the churches (except for the extremist churches like those of Father Divine and Daddy Grace), the leaders of the Nigerian churches tend to have high-flown, elaborate titles like, 'The Most Reverend Prophet Doctor Primate, Founder and Superintendent General. The leader of the Holy Ethiopian Community Church was called Chief Spirit Commander Prophet, Primate African Doctor of Divinity'. These seem more reminiscent of the Presiding Archepatriarche No. 1 than of the more usual Black church minister's designation, although acculturation – or altering of titles for outside consumption – may be at the base of some of the difference. There are also Nigerian secret societies, which Parrinder feels to be closely allied to the churches, like the

> Christian Ogboni Fraternity
> Reformed Ogboni Fraternity

where the latter is an offshoot of the former. These are perhaps even closer than the Separatist churches to the old pagan society; Parrinder specifies: 'The Reformed Ogboni leaders use titles and costumes very much like those of the old [i.e., pagan] society'.

Special attention might be called to the names Christ Apostolic Church, Christ Apostolic Gospel Church, and Saviour Apostolic Church. A kind of nucleus might be postulated as

> Christ Apostolic Church
> (1)   (2)   (3)

(Obviously, 'kernel' procedures would call for designating Apostolic Church as kernel, but such procedures seem overly ambitious in this context.) The nucleus might, then, be said to be expanded in

Christ Apostolic Gospel Church
   (1)   (2)   (X)   (3)

where X represents an expansion element. A replacement may be made in a name like

Saviour Apostolic Church
   (Y)   (2)   (3)

Lacking more detailed information, it is difficult to specify which forms derives from which other. It seems, however, possible to call one name a 'conversion' of another – or even a 'transformation', if of necessity in a much less formal sense than the most ambitious use of the term in linguistics.

In the United States, Ogboni elements are hardly obvious in the church names. The same kind of 'conversional' relationships may be seen, however, in names like

Traveling Souls Spiritual Church
   (Washington, D.C.)
Sacred Heart Spiritual Church of Jesus Christ, Inc.[22]
   (Washington, D.C.)

and many others in which Spiritual Church occurs in elaborated combinations. Or we might consider

Mount Zion Baptist Church

as a hypothetical nucleus (such a church name does occur in the Black community in Nacogdoches, Texas) and trace expansions through forms such as

Zion Travelers Baptist Church
   (Dallas, Texas)
Mount Sion Christian Spiritual Church
   (Washington, D.C.)
Mount Zion United Holy Church
   (Washington, D.C.)
First Rising Mount Zion Baptist Church
   (Washington, D.C.)
Little Zion Baptist Church No. 2
   (New Orleans)

The first thing that becomes obvious is that there is considerable mixing (perhaps 'embedding') of nuclei like

Spiritual Church

and

Mount Zion Baptist Church

The resultant names are strikingly elaborate:

Mother Bethel African Methodist Episcopal Church
  (Philadelphia)
The Old Samaritan Baptist Church
  (Washington, D.C.)
The African United Baptist Church
  (Halifax, Nova Scotia)
Gloryland Mt. Gillion Baptist Church
  (New Orleans)

For a 1968 article, I selected a corpus of ghetto storefront church names from Washington, D.C., for comparison to another corpus taken from traditional churches from the Washington metropolitan and surrounding areas, where the congregations are middle class, or mainly so, and mostly white. An attempt was made to study those names through a phrase structure analysis, primarily through the device of branching, right or left, with the word *church* (or *temple*, or any reasonable substitute) considered as head, or center. This process involves simply selecting a noun as 'head' – or nuclear component – by arbitrary if intuitively reasonable procedures and counting as 'branching' structures any components which occur to the left or to the right. Conventionally, a prepositional phrase would be considered as one component, even though consisting of three or four words; a one-word adjectival modifier of the head noun would also be considered as one component. It is, of course, possible to write more complicated 'generative' formulas; but it hardly seems necessary in the course of this discussion.

For the storefront churches, the left-branching expansion was representative of a far more numerous type. It was made of noun and other premodifiers of mainly the adjectival type, with the occurrence of other form classes not generally part of the nominal structure in Standard English. Concerning the number of pre-modifiers of the head, it can be seen that, where Standard English tends to use no more than one to three pre-modifiers, storefront churches generally use from three to five of them. The following examples are all from Washington, D.C.:

Chester Graham Rescue Mission
East Friendship Baptist Church
New Mount Nebo Baptist Church
The Old Samaritan Baptist Church

Modifications as in *New* and *First*, above, are, as will be seen from examination of any of the corpora of storefront church names presented, a regular part of the name-forming process in the Black community.

Where right-branching is concerned, great differences in usage between Black and white churches are to be found. These differences are mainly of the type in which the head of the nominal group, in the Black names, is followed by two prepositional phrases, sometimes containing as many as nine words in post-modifiers. This is clearly observable in the following:

Cannanite (sic) Temple of the Church of God
Church of God of True Holiness
The Church of God Universal Holiness No. 1
The Refuge Church of Our Lord Jesus Christ
    of the Apostolic Faith [24]

The left-branching-right-branching scheme is, obviously, not ideally conjunctive; the third example above, which is an outstanding example of right-branching, is hardly an example at all of left-branching. Nevertheless, the Black church names are strikingly longer than those of their nearest white counterparts.

It will be noted in the corpora that multiple branching is the most usual case; this may well be the source of the intuition that these practices are different from the church-naming practices of mainstream English – that they are 'exotic' or 'bizarre'. There are frequent nominal strings which not only offer three to four pre-modifiers – with the inclusion even of verb forms – but also a post-modifier consisting of two prepositional phrases. Examples are

The Holy Evangelistic Church No. 2 of North America
The Sacred Heart Spiritual Church of Jesus Christ, Inc.
Mount Calvary Holiness Church of Deliverance of the Apostolic
    Faith [25]

Bethlehem Fire Baptize Holiness Church of God of the Americans

Even the last, however, can hardly be called the champion in its genre. It must definitely take a back seat to

The United House of Prayer for All People of the Church on the Rock of the Apostolic Faith[26]

This last seems even to have a multiple head (*House* and *Church*). As might be expected, this name proved too long for actual use, and a special name – a nickname! – evolved: Daddy Grace's Church.

The traditional churches chosen for this comparison do have much more simplified names than those of the Negro storefront churches. It will be noted, particularly, that right-branching is an extremely uncommon device in such names as

Foundry Methodist Church
Cathedral of St. Peter and Paul
St. Dunstan's Episcopal Church
Walker Methodist Church
St. John's Church
Immanuel Presbyterian Church

It might be objected that the difference is between Baptist churches and Methodists, Episcopalians, etc., but any white southerner knows that Baptist churches in white communities have names like

First Baptist Church (e.g., Terrell, Texas; Nacogdoches, Texas, etc., etc.)
West Ridge Baptist Church (Grand Prairie, Texas)
Fredonia Hill Baptist Church (Nacogdoches, Texas)[27]

There are a few examples of multiple branching in any white, middle class corpus:

Langley Hill Meeting of the Religious Society of Friends

It is, however, transparently obvious that this name for a group of 'Quakers', like the terms *of Jesus Christ of Latter Day Saints* (Mormons) and *of Jehovah's Witnesses*, is an institutionalized sequence which could be entered as one unit in 'generating' the name. Although the traditional, predominantly white middle class churches display both right- and left-branching, the former is quite limited and the latter consists almost entirely of institutionalized sequences. Multiple branching is almost nonexistent, except where there are institutionalized forms on the right. Multiple branching in white churches, involves a *stereotyping* which is not matched in the Black churches. In addition, there is the factor of the obviously greater inventiveness of the Black names. Lack of inventiveness is possibly what Fairclough (1960) meant when he wrote of the 'secular' quality of the white church names. Many have been tempted to use terms like *exuberant* when considering Afro-American dialects, whether in naming practices or elsewhere. Noreen writes of the 'vitality and imagination expressed in the names of these churches', compared to which 'traditional church names of established, sophisticated denominations are somber and colorless'.

After checking hundreds of city telephone books (including those from certain cities in the South where Baptist churches, for example, were still listed under *Negro* and *White* in the mid '60's), I am inclined to believe that, insofar as *exuberant* has implications of 'spontaneous improvisation', the truth may be a more pedestrianly grammatical one. Components like *Bethel* (Church of XYZ) recur very frequently, modified into *New Bethel* (XYZ) and *Greater New Bethel* XYZ No. 2, etc. As in the case with Black English in general, the components do not differ from those of Standard English, and the other nonstandard dialects, in more than a few cases. It is the putting together, the syntax, which differs.[28] An additional, if 'lower level' grammatical difference is suggested in a few of the names provided by Noreen:

The Lord Is Able House of Prayer
Look and Live Community Church
Rise and Sun Spiritual Church

where the first, particularly, is grammatically unlike the names of middle class churches. In all three examples, the pre-modifiers are un-embedded sentences, the last two being imperatives. (The last may, however, represent an original *Rising Sun.*) It will be interesting to compare the use of the same pattern in vehicle names – or, as some would have it, mottoes. (See Chapter 4.) Low-level nonstandard grammatical patterns are seen in names like Pilgrim Progress Baptist Church (Fairclough 1960), with typical Black English possession by juxtaposition substituted for *Pilgrim's Progress.*

Fairclough's 'secularity' criterion for distinguishing white Baptist church names cannot be dismissed completely from the discussion of the Black names. He also refers to the well-known fact that white Baptist churches (especially in the South) attempt to appear as unlike the Roman Catholics as possible, avoiding all but the most common and well-known religious names. Even in those common names, the term *Saint* is anathema in a church name to white Southern Baptists. Negro churches in the same areas, on the other hand, avoid neither the name nor the idea of sainthood. Ten of the New Orleans churches whose names are presented by Fairclough commemorate saints (including a *Saint Rose* and two *Saint Mary's*). The use of saints' names for Martiniquan fishing boats (Chapter 4) might not be completely irrelevant here.

Given the distinctive secularity of the white church names and the distinctive multi-branching qualities of the Black storefront names, it seems completely unavoidable that separate traditions have been at work. The partial comparability of the African data also makes a strong suggestion, pointing in the same direction. The absence of data from the American colonial period is hardly relevant here. Perhaps the names were present, but simply not recorded. Given the well-known difficulties that slaves had in setting up and maintaining their own institutions (except under the most furtive of conditions, and almost always with some form of masking), it would not surprise us to find that the most frequently used records have simply been unrepresentative of actual conditions. It makes, however, little or no difference whether we can prove that church naming practices were in existence among the early slave communities in the Americas. The West African naming traditions are much more likely to have been manifested in the secret societies, work societies, burial societies, and lodges. Transfer of the onomastic trends to the churches would, to some degree, be a reflection of the absorption of the societies themselves in the churches.

As in other cases, the divide-and-destroy tactics which would deny Black cultural traditions by trying to subsume them in individual area patterns can be counteracted by an overview approach. In Nova Scotia, where Black English forms part of the dialect picture, names of churches and societies have apparently been as characteristic of Black culture as elsewhere. There have been

The African United Baptist Church
The Urban and Rural Life Committee
The Anglo-African Mutual Improvement and Aid Association

There are even Puerto Rican churches with names like

Iglesia Evangelista Metodista Libre, Inc. (Barrio Obrero, Santurce)

Churches, especially Pentecostal, with congregations made up of poorer Puerto Ricans, many of whom are Black, have obvious name expansions like

Iglesia Defensores de la Fé
Iglesia Defensores de la Fé Cristiana

and

Iglesia de Dios Pentecostal
Iglesia de Dios Pentecostal Las Lomas
Iglesia de Dios Pentecostal Nemesio R. Canales

(The last elements of the last two are, however, atypical of the Black pattern in that they represent a geographic location and a person commemorated, respectively.)

An Afro-American naming characteristic is thus perpetuated even in the Christian churches which presumably should have been themselves primary agents in the acculturation of Blacks to white and European traditions. It seems, then, that the kind of dynamism which is reflected in place names and in which African elements have been found to be almost entirely missing is only one kind of dynamism, although it has been studied almost to the exclusion of others. The fact that geographic elements, very frequent in white church names, are almost completely missing from Black church names is an important indication of the difference. Even if there are two churches in a Southern town, one Black and the other white, named

New Hope Baptist Church

the probability is that the white church is in a community named New Hope and that the Black church is not. The Black name, originally at least, commemorated rather the aspirations of the members than the area in which the church happened to be located.

4. Vehicle Names

The names of private cars, buses, and other vehicles provide another interesting transmission problem. The slaves who came from West Africa in the seventeenth, eighteenth, and even the early nineteenth centuries could hardly have had motor vehicles before they left Africa; therefore, it looks as if the naming practices now observable for such vehicles in Afro-America could not possibly have originated in Africa. As in the case of the church names, which may well have come from societies of other types, however, the motor vehicle names seem to represent a kind of transfer.

It is probaby significant that the same work which provides a lot of comparative material for African and Black U.S. church names, Parrinder (1953), also contains a great many examples of the type of vehicle name which was also transmitted to the New World. (The fact that Parrinder, like others, calls these 'mottoes' need not concern us immediately. The relationship between vehicle names and slogans will be dealt with below.) Although many other kinds of 'mottoes' or 'slogans' can be observed on West African vehicles, Parrinder concentrated on the religious mottoes in Nigeria:

No King as God (said to be very common)	Let them say, Trust in God
	God is good
God is God (also very common)	Christ is my hope
God be God	O give thanks unto the Lord
God is able	The Lord is mine
God save me	God first
The Lord is my shepherd	God's time
The Lord is our shepherd	God's time is the best
Trust in God[1]	God's safe journey[2]
Trust in God and do the right	*Deo gratias*

Parrinder also lists thirty-seven African-language mottoes. The trans-lations provided are such as 'Hold my hand in the shadow of death my Lord', 'The work of the Lord is easy', 'I thank the Lord King', etc.

As Parrinder and others have suggested, these look like mottoes or slogans as much as – or even more than – names. They are, at any rate, anything but mere labels. The practice of writing these – whatever they are – on buses or 'mammy wagons' is widespread in West Africa. (For obvious economic reasons, West Africans are much less likely to pos-sess private cars than the West Indians to be discussed below.) Ian Hancock has provided me with this one from Freetown, Sierra Leone:

Monkey Talk, Monkey Yeri[3]

Jan Harold Brunvand found these in West Africa:

Follow Me Number Two	Remember Me My God
People Will Talk of You	Look How God Do
Sister Girl	Oh Be Quiet

Hughes (1960) has

Repent for Death is Round the Corner	The Last Ride
	If It Must It Will
Enter Without Hope	Not Today O Lord Not Today

and Keeney (1960) has

All is Well	The Life – What You Have Done
Love Is Nice	All Shall Pass
Life Is War	

These, although they tend in the direction of being 'secular' (certainly in that not all of them are religious), are not unimaginative and by no means mere labels. Some of them may be repetitions, but the more characteristic Afro-American pattern of improvisation on a theme is more nearly what is in evidence.

In places like the West Cameroon, not even the most unobservant can keep from taking notice of these writings on buses. The AID director in Yaoundé in the mid-1960's always repeated, when the sub-ject came up, his favorite example: Always On Top, which he saw in a ditch. Schneider (1965) lists 21 of them, including

Allah De[4]	'Allah Is'
Day No Be One	'There's another day coming'

God Case, No Appeal
God De   'God Is' (God Exists)
Lagos Boy
Lefam Fo God   'Leave It to God'
Man No Be God   'Man Is Not God'[5]
Man No Rest   'Man Doesn't Rest'
Walk Fo Monin   'Walk in the Morning'

There are very many others, often in African languages. As must be obvious from the list above, religious sentiments are as likely to be expressive of Moslem as of Christian sentiments. The folk attitude of the Cameroun is that these names (or slogans, mottoes) occur 'only' in the West Cameroon. Metropolitan Yaoundé, which tries hard to be a cosmopolitan city (in 1964–1965, the government was requiring a coat of whitewash on the mud houses, and even a tin roof), likes to think that it has no such old-fashioned things. It is true that such writings on the side of buses, usually in French but sometimes in African languages and with an occasional admixture of Pidgin English, are more commonplace in smaller towns like Foumban, but I observed many such buses, with names, in Yaoundé itself.

Here are some from my East Cameroun collection:

Etoile Car
(Back: Etoile S'En Va)
Epervier
(Back: Epervier S'En Va)
Ration Car (several)
(Back: Ration S'En Va; Merci,
  Ration; Au Revoir, Ration,
  etc.)
Le Commercant
(Back: Le Commercant S'En
  Va)[6]
Raccourci No. 4
(Back: Raccourci S'En Va)
Bienvenue
(Back: Bienvenue S'En Va)
Djesse Car
(Back: Djesse S'En Va)

Laissons Tout a Dieu Faire
(Back: L'Innocent S'En Va)
Qui Sait L'Avenir
(Back: Dieu Agit Comme Il Veut
  S'En Va)
Dieu Nous Aide
(Back: Dieu d'Amour S'En Va)
L'Ombre du Plaisir du Mifi
(Back: Pacifique S'En Va)
Freres Car
(Back: Bon Voyage Freres)
Couchette de Mifi
(Back: Bon Voyage)
Bienvenue Njaleng Car
(Back: Bienvenue Njaleng Car)
Souvenir de la Soufrance
(Back: Souvenir de la Soufrance)

Bafoussam Doula   La Vie Est Un Combat No Mony
(Back: Bafoussam Douala S'En   No Playsur
Va)   (Back: La Vie Est Un Combat)

Many of these are obviously slogans (La Vie Est un Combat, No Mony
No Playsur), and few of them are religious in nature.[7] But, if these
were mottoes or slogans, why would there be the recurrence of *s'en va*
on the back? *Bienvenue* looks like just a greeting, but who would write
'Here goes Welcome' if Welcome were not a name? Ration Car, Djesse
Car, and Freres Car are perhaps labels, but Souvenir de la Soufrance
is not. Bafoussam Douala relates of course to the route of the car
(Bafoussam is a large – by Camerounian standards – town in the in-
terior, and Douala is the large port city); but Bafoussam Douala S'En
Va suggests, again, that a name has been given to the bus.

Perhaps the final word comes from spontaneous reactions of Africans, who regularly call these names. While I was traveling across the
border from the Cameroun to Nigeria to attend the fourth annual con-
ference of the West African Language Survey, my traveling companion,
Professor Henri Marcel Bot-ba-Njock of the Université Federale du
Cameroun, and I saw, just inside Nigeria, a bus with AMEN written
across the front. Professor Bot-ba-Njock's reaction was spontaneous,
'Cette voiture s'appele AMEN!'

Many examples occur from outside West African territory. Jan
Knappert, who has been kind enough to give me several from his collection, is among the many sharp observers who have been struck by
these names. He cites the following examples and explanations from
Swahili, the lingua franca of East and Central Africa:

Leo si kehso   'Today is not tomorrow'
(Normally this means do not worry for tomorrow, but here it
refers to the passengers who says: I will pay tomorrow.)
Nipe changu   'Give me my due'
(This has the same implication, but the added note for amusement
is that it is a variant on what prostitutes are supposed to say to
their customers.)
Nijaribu tena   'Let me try again'
(This may refer to the many breakdowns on the African roads,
but it can also be another phrase used by a prostitute, equivalent
to 'Try me again'.)
Rudi nami   'Come back with me, too'
(The same set of implications.)

Kwenda na kurudi	'Going and coming back'

(This means that the bus line has plenty of business.)

Halambee	'Forward'
Bisumila	'In God's Name'
Taratibu	'Be Careful'
Safari Salama	'Safe Journey'
Hongera	'Success'
Kwenda kwa salama	'Go in peace'
Usife njiana	'Do not die on the road'
Sipende hatari	'Do not love danger'

(This indicates that the trip is hazardous.)

Lipa leo	'Pay today'

(This expresses the Islamic attitude that tomorrow is Judgment Day, too late to pay one's debts.)

Ya leo	'(The business) of Today'

(This has the same implication.)

Ajuaye	'He that knows (is God)'
Atuweke	'May He keep us'
Ndije mpaji	'He is the Giver'
Mpende Nduguyo	'Love thy brother'

(This is also a way of urging drivers to be careful.)

Mwenzangu	'My friend'
Usinisahau	'Do not forget me'
Kwanza kwa salama	'Start in peace'
Kwisha kwa salama	'End in peace'

Professor Knappert (personal communication) feels that these are all proverbs, although he also refers to them as 'bus names' and feels that they 'fulfill a special function' in Africa that we have not yet sounded in depth. My own experience agrees with both of these conclusions, but I would wish to extend Professor Knappert's phrase 'in Africa' to 'in Afro-America'.

The two Swahili vehicle names which I was able to collect in Burundi both have slogan-like or proverbial qualities. Ndege ruka 'the plane or bird flies' seems to have the connotation 'I speed along like a bird (or plane)'. Professor Knappert finds that it evokes the Flemish proverb, 'Falcon, fly', which refers to the struggle for freedom of that people. The other Burundi name was Wacheni Fitina 'leave off jealousy' (don't be jealous). On the front bumper of a truck, it expressed the driver's superiority over his earth-bound fellows. But one of the many horribly deformed polio victims who wheeled their chairs around Bujumbura, begging from Europeans, had written *Wacheni Fitina* on the back of his own vehicle. One would hardly call the emotion expressed arrogance.

The names of buses and other vehicles can also be found throughout the Caribbean and other parts of Afro-America, in French (or French Creole) and English (sometimes Creole-tinged), and to some degree in other languages.[8] As might have been expected, the greatest concentration of them is in Haiti, where African survivals are known to be abundant.[9] Names (or slogans) on Haitian *camionettes* are so abundant, in Port-au-Prince, that only the constant intervention of would-be guides restricts the number which one can collect in a single day. Unfortunately, the same conviction that any outsider is a tourist and must be seeking wine, women, and song (or perhaps imitation native Haitian handcrafts) renders the ability to sample native intuition about the names/mottoes/slogans much more difficult than it is in West Africa. It must be admitted, however, that some suspicion of name-collecting activity is likely to arise anywhere.[10] In spite of these limitations, however, I collected the following in a few days in Port-au-Prince. A few were supplied to me, and interpretations given, by Haitian academics.[11]

La Fourmi	Choupette
La Joie de Vivre	Merci Reine (Back: Saut de
En Plein Air	l'Eau)
L'Eternel Est Tout Puissant	Pleut Pour Toi (Back: Ne Pleut
Voici Ti Joseline	Pas Pour Moi)
La Lumiere du Soleil	La Voila
Dieu L'Avenir	Enfant de la Veuve
Ocupe A Fait Pa Ou	Delta
M'Ap Mete e Main	Destin
A La Douce	Toujours Ste Rose (Back: Dieu
Tout la Volonte de Dieu	Est Bon)
Ce Lavie (a pushcart)	Merci St. Joseph
Le Fils du Bon Berger	Boule de Feu
Moin Pa Ou, Voisin	La Bienveillance
Effort et Volonte	Dieu L'A Voulu (Back: Nap
Le Travail Est la Loi du Monde	Mete Main)
L'Exactitude (front)	Dieu L'Avenir
Toi et Moi, Cheri (back)	La Prudence de Alta Gracia[13]

Fok Nan Poin

Buscando La Vida[12]

Toujours M Nan Mitan Yo

L'Oeil du Maitre

Min Bon Materiaux
  (ice cream cart)

Champion

Toujours au Travail

Dieu a Voulu (Back: Bob)

Voici Marcel

Qui Perd Gagne

Rose & Jacques (Back: Rose:
  La Reine des Fleurs)

La Belle Port-au-Princienne

La Violetera

La Vie

La Vie Drole

Sans Crainte

Merci Notre Dame

Reine du Ciel

Quand Meme

Me Voila

Mete Cran

Dieu Qui Donne

Doulette

Frankie

Cheleina

Angelique[14]

Maria

Marie Jose

Gaby

Angelita

These Haitian *camionette* names have always impressed me as being very similar to those of the East Camerounian mammy wagons, although no stratement about geographic origin or direct transmission is thereby implied. Even the vehicles – Renault minibuses – are the same. The Haitians seem, if anything, more optimistic in the attitudes which they express; and their poverty, at least as extreme as that of the West Africans, would not seem to justify such hopefulness. The explanation may be that a driver of a bus in Haiti, as a salaried worker, is so much better off than the average Haitian that he can afford to indulge in expressions of superiority. It is perhaps this factor which causes a Haitian driver to proclaim to the world: *Weep For Yourself; Don't Weep For Me* at the same time that he admits *Work Is the Law of the World*. Even the pushcart *C'Est La Vie* is more optimistic than its counterpart in Nkongsamba, East Cameroun: *En Lieu de Chomer*. 'That's Life' is, after all, a more optimistic philosophy than 'Oh, well, it beats loafing around'.

From other officially French-speaking[15] islands of the Caribbean, it is almost equally easy to find such names. In Guadeloupe, in 1964, I collected

Moin Aigri (twice)

Toute Suite [sic]

Mystere

Corntiky [sic] II

Voila
Mi Amor I [16]
Mi Amor II
Mi Amor III
La Providence II
Patience

L'Ombre
Aux Doux Sourire
Destin II
St. Cristophe
Perseverance

A return trip, in 1974, netted

Mi Amor
Probleme

Beau Soleil

The number collected, even in a longer stay, was fewer in 1974, and impressionistically it did seem true that there were fewer such bus names. Continuity, however, does seem to be indicated.

In the officially English-speaking islands of the Caribbean, the same kinds of naming traditions seem to have been at work. These are, of course, not always buses. In Roseau, Dominica, I found (as in parts of Africa, like Burundi) personnel carrier trucks rather than buses. They had names like

Lady Ruthine
Lady Carmine

Sugar Pie

which admittedly look as much like European as African naming patterns. An occasional Jamaican taxi name, like Teddy Bear, has been reported to me, although no real collection seem to have been made there. On St. Thomas, taxis (sometimes driven by 'aliens', immigrants from down-island) sometimes have names like

Big Red Cobra
Mr. Macreamanus

Ding Aling Taxi (an old Volkswagen)

On the smaller island of St. John, taxi names are even easier to find:

Mother's Love
Lover's Prayer
Calaloo

Look at Me
Sand in My Shoes

In all the U.S. Virgin Islands, names of this sort can be seen painted on the sides of cars. Not all of them are as elaborately painted as *Loves Me No One* (Christiansted, St. Croix), but many of them are so attractively presented as to give evidence of the owner's care in lettering and painting. Some of them follow:

Boopsie	Nigger Charlie
Trouble Man[17]	Love Bug[19]
Baby Shaf[18]	Mr. Lightning
Sad Mover	The Different
Apollo II	Buccaneer
Consider Me	Rated X

The last has a picture of a handsome but scornful young Black with three girls kneeling before him in a posture of supplication. Residents of St. Thomas assure me that X-rated pictures do not come there, but the inhabitants are hardly cut off from the outside world. Sporadic reports from other islands include a minibus from St. Kitts named Lady Jackson and one from St. Martin named Queen Anne.

Any of the owners of the cars observed on St. Croix, especially, may be of Puerto Rican ancestry. Puerto Ricans on their own island, furthermore, especially those of the lower socio-economic class, have a marked tendency to write names or slogans on their vehicles. Trucks and private cars have

Muñeca (truck, front bumper)	El Bohemio Alegre
El Poderoso (a *big* truck)	Gold Duster
El Pinto (a Toyota, 'painted' with rust remover)	Red Diamond
	The Judge
El Avispon Velde [sic – reflecting dialect phonology for *verde*]	Captain Guts
	Mr. Magu
	La Paloma
Cordero (truck, front mud flap)	El Piau
Carrito El Chévere (a piragua cart)	Condenado a la Distancia

But perhaps the most significant of them all was that of a jitney-car *(público)*, driven by a Black Puerto Rican: El Chucho Train 'The Pussy Wagon', with some attempt, especially in the use of the spelling *Train* rather than *Tren*, to mask the obscenity by suggesting English *choo choo train*.

The decal advertising campaigns of commercial automobile manufacturers have had very significant success in Puerto Rico, so that many automobiles are marked (in large letters, usually over a back wheel)

DUSTER, PINTO, MACH I, COLT, CRICKET (suspectible to obscene interpretation, especially when pronounced without final -*t*, which is of course the usual pronunciation of a native Puerto Rican), COUGAR, CAMARO, NOVA, and SUPER BEE. It seems very likely that something like the Afro-American car naming pattern has been essentially absorbed by a commercial pattern with which it has overlapping features.

Added to this is the fact that many Puerto Ricans have found a novel way to project mottoes/slogans. Puerto Rico requires only one private automobile license plate, on the back, leaving the front holder available for other use. Many take advantage of the space for messages, largely religious and sometimes rather ingenious. An owner of a Chevrolet El Camino thus tells the world 'Cristo Es El Camino' by this method. Most, however, are less clever, like 'Soy Cristiano, Mi Amor Es Jesucristo'. Although a majority of such slogans are religious, others are political in import. Puerto Ricans frequently put stickers saying 'Esto 'Ta [Esta] Malisimo', referring to the current admiinstration, on their windows and windshields. Messages or names may be in English, often with the influence of Spanish orthography (e.g., Mr. Magu, for the movie cartoon character Mr. Magoo). A pushcart fruit vendor on Calle Loiza in virtually all-Puerto Rican Barrio Obrero had scrawled 'Come 'n' Get It' on the side of his vehicle.[20]

Minibus *públicos*, which start from the plaza of Río Piedras and go to all parts of the island, are popularly believed to have many such mottoes painted on them. In this, my informants reversed the usual trend. There were actually fewer such slogans than they asserted. In several trips around the plaza I found only 'El Orgullo Tambien Muere' and 'El Mio No Se Desgaste'. The second is, however, a cliché; only the first shows possible expression of the philosophy or sentiments of the owner or driver. Commercially sold stickers (like the second) are rather common on vehicles in the same general area. One, which pictures a large-billed bird over the words

> Por que me sigues?
> (Sic – without the usual initial inverted question mark of Spanish punctuation.)

With the possible exception of the Puerto Rican examples, such materials increasingly become names rather than mottoes or slogans as we move from West Africa, through Haiti, and into the West Indian islands. The process has gone even further in the United States, where

Black owners of vehicles write on them things like

The Lost Sheep (a truck in New York City)
Titty Pink[21]
Big Mack (a truck in New York City)
The Julie John (a car, in Nacogdoches, Texas)

Car names from the Adams-Morgan community of Washington, D.C., include

Chevvy Deuce (obviously, a Chevy II)
Boss Bat
Faith Chariot

The 'Africanism' of the names becomes a moot point by this time. It might be observed, however, that Europeanization (or Americanization) is most extreme at just those places where acculturation has otherwise been most complete. The Herskovitsian theory holds, however, that acculturation was never complete. The 'bizarreness' or 'exoticism' of names like The Lost Sheep (particularly when it is considered in conjunction with ghetto church names, discussed in the last chapter), coupled with the marked tendency to project personal characteristics rather than a tribute to a wife, daughter, or girl friend[22] seems to make it meaningful to suggest that there has been such a pattern of West African naming practices with progressive acculturation.

There is, obviously, reason to object – to quibble over the difference between an originally European pattern and an African pattern which has become 'Europeanized'. I feel that the bus, truck, and automobile names in the continental United States reveal vestigial traces of patterns which cannot be explained in terms of European naming practices. In places like Haiti, the relationship is more clear cut and can even be expressed in terms of African survivals. There is, however, a more trivial objection which can be more easily dealt with. On a superficial level of history, it is easy to point out that the slaves had no motor vehicles during the period of their being carried to the New World. It can, then, be argued that the Blacks of the New World got their motor vehicles – and, therefore, the naming tradition for them – from Europeans. This is a very simplistic argument, but it has been frequently advanced. The argument that Blacks simply took over European languages, which has been the bone of contention in the Creolist-dialect geographer controversy,[23] is also a critical part of this argument.

Against the technological argument, it seems fairly significant that the West Africans have naming/motto-giving traditions which are not restricted to motor or wheeled vehicles – or even to vehicles.[24] West African fishermen, for example, frequently record mottoes or slogans on the sides of their canoes. The International Development Research Centre Annual Report for 1972–1973 shows, quite incidentally as a part of its report on 'Ghana Fisheries', an elaborately painted 'native' canoe with the name God is King (p. 29). This may, of course, be rather an expression of a personal philosophy; on the cabin of the rather large boat is also painted 'Work And Happiness'. More traditional fishing boats, shown on the preceding page of the report, have elaborate symbols painted on them and may in some way express the same kind of philosophy. There is also a beautiful example in the drawings of John Biggers (*Ananse, The Web of Life in Africa*).[25] The drawing, of a boat used by Fante fishermen, is accompanied by the explanation:

> Proverbs and symbols expressing the philosophy of each boat crew adorn the sides. Delicately carved in low relief, they are painted in bright reds, brilliant yellows, and deep greens. The hull is black (p. 36).

The use of artistic effects, including elaborate letters and bright colors, in the rendering of such names, slogans, or mottoes is also characteristic of the vehicle names so far described for West Africa and for the Caribbean, and to a slightly lesser degree in those of the continental United States. It is somewhat less pronounced for the truck names of Burundi, but the names themselves are much less frequent there.

In the West Indies, fishermen also give such names/slogans to their boats. The most important and most nearly exhaustive study of such patterns is that of Richard and Sally Price, in spite of their modest title 'A Note on Canoe Names in Martinique'.[26] Price and Price record twenty-two canoes named after saints (with eight for St. Michel and two for St. Simon), probably because 'fishermen pray to their patron saints in front of household chromolithographs before going to sea each morning'.[27] St. Michel, who 'is locally recognized as the vanquisher of demons' is more popular than St. Pierre, even though the latter is the biblical patron of fishermen, because St. Michel provides both protection and a bountiful catch. There are other religious names like

Apres Dieu	Dieu Qui Ma Donne
Confiance en Dieu	Reconnaissance a Dieu
Dieu Commande	Volonté de Dieu

Price and Price call these names without hesitation, although obviously from a content point of view they could as easily be called slogans or mottoes.[28] Certain others, however, are given the names of people; and the tradition is thus as little distinguishable from European traditions as the above are from general Catholic traditions:

Alice	Sylvina
Mili	Yvonne

The interesting names from the Price and Price collection, from the point of view of the present discussion, are those called 'Other Secular Names'. Again, they are rather marginal in that they could as easily be called mottoes:

Laisses Yo Dit	1er Amour
La Jeunesse Belle Messieu	Quand Meme[29]
La Patience	Reine Sans Peine
Le Jour Est Arrive	Revanche a Mes Parents

All in all, Price and Price list thirty-three such names; and there are other, even more interesting ones, which they recorded as 'Initial Names'.

These last, of which Price and Price elicited interpretations from the owners, seem even more like the West African slogans/mottoes:

C. A. Q. F. C A C.D. LAR D . . .	MPS
(Ça qui fait ça a cent dolars)	(ma passion)
E. de M. P. B.	S. V. G.
(enfant de malheur, bonne prosperité)	(no interpretation provided)

The use of initials for a more traditional West African-type pattern would not be unexpected, since the general reaction is that such patterns are 'old-fashioned', and the owners may have feared ridicule – or the annoyance of novelty-seeking outsiders who wanted to gawk at or collect the names. Price and Price also record the interesting information that

The fisherman who believes himself 'bewitched' often changes the name of his craft to confuse the forces of evil, usually with the assistance of a professional consultant, and when a second hand canoe is purchased, its name is almost always changed.[30]

The name shifting, documented above for personal names, is, therefore, apparently a part of the canoe-naming practice. (It would, of course, change the description very little to substitute *motto* or *slogan* for *name*.)

Bush Negroes of the interior of Surinam also give names to their canoes, many of them being fish names.[31]

Kwie-Kwie	'sweet water'
Mofina	'poverty'
Wai Na Pasi	'Get Out of the Way'
Mi Na Ten	'I Am Time'
Marianna	
Juliana	
Me Doe [32]	
Mi Kon Fo Doe	'I Come/Came to Do'
Koemaroe	
Kwana	
Warakoe	
Yeke Yeke	
Toekoenai	Names of a fish
Ma Lokko	
Sriba	
Pito	

It is reported that Indians in the interior of Suriname sometimes name their boats Kanawa, which simply means 'boat' or 'canoe'.[33]

In Basseterre, St. Kitts, the following were found:

Fear Not	Faithful
Lady Marina	Faithful Promise
Neater	Hummingbird
Florence	Colony Boy
Come Again	Yankee Boy
Albatross	If
Caribbean Cloud	Magdala
Some Joy	Michelyn
Decasela	Irish Town

Adina	Old Road
Stranger Youth	Gwendolyn
Thunderbird	Ebinite
The Black Witch	Ethel
Vanguard	Help Me
Flipper	Sympathy
Ramona	Sweet Sixteen
KLM	Clayvis
Patient	Bernardine
Bismark	Stay Up
Let Them Say	Eileen
Greenland	Excelsior
Honolulu	Duel
Skylark	Deliverance
Navy Blues	Ambow
Ranger	Amstel
Sea Hawk	Lady Williams
Love God	Yes
Nelson	DLB
Lady Bratwater	Student
Kelly	Girl Woodley
Marvella	Worries [34]

On the waterfront in Charlotte Amalie, St. Thomas, there are canoes with names like

Geneva	Delay
Jennifer	Mary Jane

These look as assimilated as names can be – the last was actually the example which I had used in academic discussions for what a European-type boat name would be. On the other side of the prow of the same rather battered little canoe, however, is a rather more typically Afro-American element:

To See Miss Mary Jane

Elsewhere, there have been scattered collections. A newspaper picture provides a view of the High Sea Worrier [sic] from Anguilla.[35] Boats in the harbor and nearby at Point-à-Pitre, Guadeloupe are named Les Algues and Beau Garçon – to stick only to small native canoes. A larger boat, big enough to be ocean-going, has Siuvez [sic] Moi Les Marins written, with the same spelling in each case, on the back and side. Another larger one appears to be named Marie des Indes (back and side). The General Dugommier, however, is a passenger ship probably operated for the tourist trade and thereby does not qualify for inclusion here.

The argument that Black slaves transferred their traditional boat-naming practices to wheeled vehicles is buttressed by historical records which provide some examples of slaves who owned boats and gave 'exotic' names to them. In the Jamaican *Tom Kringle's Log* (c. 1833), Jamaican boatmen are represented as owning small sailboats, in which they carry passengers. The boats have names like

> Pam Be Civil[36]   De Monkey
> Ballahoo   Stamp-and-Go[37]

There seems to be no historical – and probably no geographic break. John McNamara collected the following names of Virgin Islands bumboats in 1940:

> Flower of Syria   Star of the East
> Hood

There is evidence of canoe naming in Gullah territory; given the recently established importance of Gullah in matters of American Negro language and culture,[38] there is reason to believe that the practice might shed some light on the practices of Negroes in other parts of the United States. Gonzales, in *The Black Border*, points out

> On the seacoast and along the lower reaches of the tidal rivers, 'trus'-me-Gawd' (I trust my God) is the common name for the cranky, unseaworthy dugout canoe, the hazard of whose use on the rough waters of the coast implies faith in the watchful care of a divine providence.[39]

Common name, for Gonzales, possibly means no more than common noun;[40] but, whether he realized it or not, such information may be comparable to the way in which the day names became common nouns in Jamaican. Gonzales refers to the same name elsewhere,[41] and it seems plausible that the historical change in the Low Country has been in the direction of proper noun to common noun.[42]

Gullah expert William A. Stewart further informs me that a fifteen-year-old Gullah informant (from Edisto Island) reports no current practice of canoe naming but does remember a rowboat which bore the words 'In God We Trust'. This looks like a slogan, based on the national slogan of the United States; but it is a slogan which reveals the underlying influence of the older canoe names and which is directly paralleled by a Jamaican cart.[43] Possibly the Gullah boat-owner saw the words on a coin, but the slogan was reinforced (and the impulse to use it as a boat designation was undoubtedly determined) by the older canoe naming practice. The Caribbeanist – among whom should be counted ideally workers on Gullah – is fully accustomed to working with reinforcements from one tradition to another, and the problem actually becomes somewhat simpler to him. There is no conflict, likewise, between sloganeering and naming, but a reinforcement of one by the other.

From the early colonial period, Blacks played a very important role in the water life of the continental colonies and the United States. Wood, *Black Majority*, describes how

> From the start they tended, along with the local Indians, to dominate the fishing of the region, for Englishmen, while capable of hauling nets at sea from an ocean-going vessel, were not at home in a dugout canoe.[44]

Further, slaves often served on merchantmen at sea.[45] Inland, they frequently worked on Mississipi river boats. On those boats, jazz bands formed by Black musicians like Fate Marabel found some of the first places where they could secure employment, and Black traditions began to have their influence on more whites than just the master's family on the plantation. For steamboats, with names well known to folklore and tradition like the Robert E. Lee and the Natchez, there seems to be rather little that could represent any kind of Black – much less 'African' – tradition. But there is evidence, again, that the workmen, who were mostly Negroes,[46] had their own unofficial naming tradition:

> Many boats were known by the nicknames given them by the rousters. For example, the W. A. Johnson was known during her lifetime as the 'Pig Iron Johnson'. The reason for this title was the large quantity of pig iron the vessel carried to Paducah and Evansville from the furnace in La Grange.[47]

Wheeler goes on to point out how the packet Stacker Lee[48] was given various other nicknames which were 'invented by the Negroes for the packet'; The Stack, The Big Smoke, Stack o'Dollahs, Bull of the Woods, and various other nicknames. They had the name The Peanut John for a steamboat which was officially known as the John Gilbert; the Lovin' Kate for the Kate Adams (the third by that name); the Jim Lee for the James Lee. One, the official name for which is not provided, was called Tobin's Train by the Black rivermen.[49]

Names of the steamboats, further, figured heavily in the songs of the Blacks on the river. For the Stacker Lee, there was the couplet

If the Stack don't drown
I'm Alabama bound.[50]

for the Robert E. Lee

Shoo, fly, don't bother me (three times)
I'se workin' on de Lee[51]

and for still another

There's a big boat, a-mmm', it's got no name
But the boys all call it the Paul Tulane, oh Babe.[52]

Thus, even assuming that the official names of the steamboats had no influence from the Blacks who made up most of their crews, there is much reason to believe that the association between slaves and their descendants and the naming of river, ocean, and stream vehicles was never completely stifled.

Thus, there is evidence from vehicle and boat names that Blacks never came to the point of merely adopting an onomastic system which was purely European in origin. Whether this means survivals of Africanisms in any narrow sense or rather the persistence of 'hybrid' patterns which developed in contact is not really a critical matter in this context. What does seem to be highly likely is that not only did the Black practices not consist entirely of imitations of European and American practices but that the former actually exercised some influence on the latter.

5. Shops, Vendors, and Things for Sale

The last stage of the transfer from West African cultural patterns to Afro-American cultural patterns, with the obvious absorption of European elements all along the way, must have been the naming of shops and places of business. Very few of the slaves could, obviously, have owned businesses; but we find early references to enterprising slaves who had set themselves up in transportation (canoes, etc.) and other businesses.[1] It is well known that some of the plantation slaves were able to raise enough vegetables on the plots of land granted to them by the owners not only to feed themselves but even to sell to outsiders and to make a little bit of money.[2] Somewhere along the way, at least by the time the descendants of West Africans were freedmen, a tradition of keeping small shops – and of naming them – had grown up.[3]

Although the visitor to Buea, West Cameroon, may miss these names if he sticks to the European side of things, a short walk into Buea Town (where many knowing friends had warned me no white man dared set foot but where I received only smiles and courteous greetings), turned up these names:[4]

The City of Fountain Pens (a sidewalk show case)
Rainbow Patent Medicine Store
Golden Photo Studio
The Famous Independent Machine Bread Industry
Cameroun Hope Rising Bar
A Little House of No Regret (a tailor)
We We Cabinet Store
The Acrobat City Radio Doctor
Miss Anna's Modern Fancy Store

Elsewhere in the Cameroun, as at Haut-Nkom, I observed names like

Jeunesse Bar de Haut-Nkom
Mamies Jolies Bar
Le Bonne Future (a restaurant)

Cameroun Hope Rising is a moderate name for a bar compared to the one reported in Accra by F. N. Keeney:

Kalamazoo Shake Your Head[5]

Elsewhere, there are names to be found like La Vida Rica[6] in Santa Isabel, Fernando Poo, and La Joie de Vivre in Douala – both of them bars. In Douala also, I observed La Terre Tourne, a grocery store, and El Domino, another bar in the same city. Like the problematic things written on vehicles and churches, some of these could as easily be called slogans or mottoes as names, although most of us tend to assume more easily that a store has a name and not something else. The champion insofar as length goes, however, was obviously a name, on a store in Haut-Nkom:

La Maison La Plus Moins Cher Pour Les Tissues En Metres

The championship in exoticism and bizarreness, however, must go to a small shop in Nkongsamba:

God With Us And Sons[7]

Apart from the Pidgin English work naming tradition, the last name can not be explained – makes, perhaps, no sense at all. Once we know, however, what kinds of names Cameroonians who leave their native village take for themselves (see Chapter 1), then we find a ready explanation. God With Us has left his home village and taken that name expressing religious sentiments (whether Christian or Moslem we are not likely to find out). Having gone into business for himself and had some success, he later takes his sons in as partners. Thus, God With Us and Sons is a direct parallel to Smith and Sons or Jones and Sons. The bizarreness is, as usual, in the eye of the beholder; but it is a predictable reaction in a European or American who is exposed to the name for the first time.

It is very likely that, as vehicle names are to be found all along the West African coast, so the striking store names must be found in the same areas. I have not, unfortunately, been able to do the same kind of collecting for the latter; and the literature available from observers, no matter how casual, is by no means so extensive. It is easy to remember the sidewalk watch repair shops in Bujumbura, with names like Horlogerie du Congo, which make us think of DeCamp's remark about how West Indians love naming things.[8] It would appear that the watch repairman obtained a few tools (and, hopefully, some expertise in repair), then a small table which could serve as shop during the day and be removed at night, and then immediately thereafter a name for his 'establishment'.

In the Americas, too, collection has been much more sporadic. Port-au-Prince is, again, the happy hunting ground; but the abundance of self-appointed tourist guides, perfectly certain that a white male wandering around alone must be looking for female companionship, constitutes a great handicap. In spite of this, in addition to Boulangerie Du Bon Berger and Texaco Station De L'Etoile Rouge, I collected the following names of shops which sold Bôlette (also spelled Borlette and Bolette) tickets:

Dieu Si Bon	Bolette of Elia 50-15-10
Rapidite	Bolette Au Gout Du Cliente
Ofelia	Die Ca Ou Vle Voisin
El Ballo	AVIE (Perhaps A Vie, for Fran-
Atlas	çois Duvalier, just 'appointed'
Mercure	president for life)
Good Luck	Fortuna
Bolette Bar Tonnere	Satellite
St. Ives	Bolette Treinta Y Tres
Pescado Rojo	El Amigo Borlette
Bolette Cine Lado	C'Est Mon Etoile
Etoile De La	

The occasional name on a vendor's box (Doc A Vie, in commemoration of the elevation of Duvalier to lifetime 'president') on the wooden container from which a Haitian sold cigarettes and candy in the old Port-au-Prince airport can be paralleled from many experiences in Africa and from The Poor Boy on a shoe shine purveyor's box in New York City. This last is, obviously, the same kind of self-ironic commentary as the various African and Jamaican carts with names purporting 'It's not much, but it's necessary'.[9]

In Paramaribo, Surinam, where urban environment clashes with lack of acculturation to the delight of the name collector, there are

Barber Shop Americano

Las Vegas Barber Shop

Kansas City Barber Shop

Success Radio Service

Palmtree Store

Tutti Frutti/Toeti Froeti Bar

In God We Trust (a pension)

The names are in English rather than in Sranan Tongo, but this is not inconsistent with the practices of a country where the most authentic folksinger is named Big Jones. It was there, also, that the breakfast menu in my hotel advertised 'Selectable French Toast'.

On an island like St. Croix, apart from the tourist-oriented stores and bars which have an exoticism all their own (e.g., The Stone Balloon), we can find Christiansted bars with names like

Busy-Bee Pool Room

Davy Jone's [sic] Locker Bar and Rest.

Ringside, Corner Bar (with a painting of a boxer) Kid Tough, Prop.

The Calabash Bar Lounge

De [sic] Hive

V. I. [Virgin Islands] Palm Bar and Poolroom

Weeke's Ten Grand Bar and Restaurant[10]

Wringer Room Bar

Baron Spot Christiansted[11]

Fallen Star Bar and Restaurant

And other establishments have names like

Happy Corner (Roast Pork)

Dodie's Sun and Moon Fashions

Hummingbird Laundromat

Horn of Plenty Market

Top Banana Vegetable and Pro-
    vision Store

Foreign Tailors

Jerusalem Store

United Furniture Home Appli-
    ance Household

Charlotte Amalie, St. Thomas, is as touristy and commercial as a town can be, but we still find native bars with names like

Hummingbird Bar Pool Room

The Powder Horn Tavern

Purple Manor Bar

Names of this type for small stores, at any rate, spread to the Bahamas at an early date. In 1942, John McNamara, a long-time worker with the American Name Society, collected the following:

The Go Slow Butcher Shop
God Promise to Help (a bar)
Jehovah Jireh – Dry Goods and
   Notions
Weary Willy's Inn

Percival Veau
   Licensed to sell
   Butcher's Meat
Rudolph Widderbunn &
   Bertram Bowleg

Fictional sources, particularly those of Black writers, provide at least some evidence of the existence of such store and bar names in the continental United States. William Melvyn Kelley's Joycean *Dunford's Travels Everywhere* refers to ghetto bars like

The Johnson Jones Jail House
B.Q.'s
Hare's Lair
The Brown Turtle
Jesse B's Joyce Club
Brown's

Mr. Mitey's Blessed Diner
Melvin's Jazzmatazz Gallery
Smokey's Smother Room
Rinehart's Restaurant
TM's Dream Room
Sonny R's Boom Bar

Toni Morrison's *Sula* (1974) has the Time and a Half Pool Hall, the Elmira Theatre, Irene's Palace of Cosmetology, Edna Finch's Mellow House – all in the small fictional town of Medallion. Ishmael Reed's satirical *The Last Days of Louisiana Red*, somewhat more cosmopolitan in locale, has the Solid Gumbo Works. Reed's satirical bent, which leads to such onomastic high jinks as a course at Berkeley called The Jaybird as an Omen in Afro-American Folklore and a white literature named Maxwell Kasavuba, also features The Dahomeyan Softball Team and Rev. Rookie of the Gross Christian Church.

In other Black literature, such names occur frequently. In Iceberg Slim's *Pimp, The Story of My Life*, the characters occasionally eat at places like The Roost and Creole Fat's Rib Heaven. A more important work, Ralph Ellison's *The Invisible Man*, has an important scene at a bar-brothel named The Golden Day Bar. Carson McCullers, whose *The Heart Is a Lonely Hunter* features Black characters named Highboy and June Bug, sets important action in Madame Reba's Palace of Sweet Pleasure.

Shops, bars, and restaurants will remain, however, basically marginal to any treatment of Black names. The people who came to the Americas in chains notoriously did not make their sales from shops which they themselves owned – and therefore could give their official names. Pushcarts and boats (already treated in Chapter 2) were more nearly the establishments they sold from.

The things they sold, on the other hand, were somewhat more susceptible to being made to the slaves' own order. Possibly the most important thing which they sold – more important than females' bodies in Storyville or even the jazz which started from such places as Storyville and spread to the bars and concert stages of the nation – was the set of beliefs and techniques associated with root magic. The supposedly medicinal herbs, effective really only when combined with conjuration, were sold among the Blacks themselves and not mainly to outsiders. Nevertheless, that commerce may have been, in sheer magnitude, the greatest of them all.[12]

The terminology of the root 'doctors' is, not unexpectedly, unfamiliar and even lurid to generations conditioned to the drugstore. The roots have names like the long familiar John the Conqueror (de Conker), in the guise of either Low John de Conker or High John de Conker. They are Hearts Cologne, Red Devil Lye, Hearts Perfume, or

Van Van	Sensitive Brier
Devil's Shoe String	Shame Face
Chinese Wash	Shame Jim
Mustard Seed	Shamin' Judy
The Nine Herbs from Cincinnati	Shoe-Tongue Root
Deadman Root	Ruler of de Worl'
Shame Brier	Spirit of Jesus
Shame Vine	

The complete story of root and conjure magic has not been told, nor has a really impressive beginning on such a story been made. The material is, probably, just too foreign – too different from what the rather timid historians of American culture have grown accustomed to dealing with and developed any competence in. The nearest approach has been made in a great, sprawling, disorganized five-volume collection by Harry Middleton Hyatt.[13] In that work, we can read of Dr. E. D. England, M.A., Famous Mentalist, who offered for sale (from his address in Norfolk, Virginia)

Zandro's Good Luck Incense Race	Clearing House Dream Incense, Large Size[14]
Wall Street Dream	Temple of Solomon
Zandro's High Power Dream	Mystic Initiation

Combination	Temple of Moses
Zodiac Incense	England Love Mystic
England Luck Oil	

Dr. England, who wears a turban in the picture on his business card (reproduced by Hyatt) is nevertheless obviously an American of West African ancestry. So is the Eld. Father Caffrey, Christlike Spiritual Temple. So was the Rt. Rev. Bosinson, L.L., D.D., who boasted 'No Roots Is Used – No Witchcraft Is Used' from his address in St. Petersburg, Florida. Hyatt's clear intuition was that these men were working in the same tradition as Prophet Warkiee Sarheed, who announced himself to be 'from Ghana, Africa', and who also wore a turban. The tradition of African transmission is strong in root magic; the symbolic truth, at least, of such statements of origin is very great.

Other rootwork 'doctors' whom Hyatt interviewed were called Daddy Snakelegs, Jack of Diamonds, Dr. Yousee, 'Hustlin' Woman', Nahnee 'Boss of Algiers', Doctor Buzzard, Madam Pauline, 'The Jack Ball Man', Havana Man, Doc. There may be considerable significance in the resemblance of these names to other nicknames in Black American culture (cf., for an obvious case, Jelly Roll Morton's title 'Doctor Jazz') since rootwork magic may be a kind of 'basilect' cultural factor.

The depth of rootwork magic has not been plumbed, nor are there more than sketchy indications of its geographic spread. Even Herskovits and Herskovits (1936: 99–103) give few details about the herbs themselves used in Surinam; it may be, however, that the herb work itself grows in complexity as the clearly religious implications of obeah decline. Certainly, the Virgin Islands have a rich herb and name lore. The excellent little book by Arona Petersen, *Herbs and Proverbs of the Virgin Islands* (1974) provides an explicit statement of what many feel about these matters: 'You will note the African flavor in many of the sayings.'[15] And, again, it is probably significant that Petersen chose to combine names of herbs and proverbs – on opposing pages. The names, some of which are like slogans (Man-better-man), include the following:

Stack-Ma-Hark, or Cat's Blood	Pigeon Peas Bush
Love Bush	Pissy Bed Bush
Moon Plant	Tan-Tan
Old Maid Stinking Toe	

Puerto Rico is also a place where the ingredients of root magic can be bought in *botánicas*, especially those which contain the element *La Fé de* . . . in their names. It is a place which has a Floristeria Shango, obviously named after the vodun thunder god.[16] *Espiritismo* is the great unacknowledged religion of the common people, especially of the Black segment centered in the Loiza-Carolina area. The barmaids of Río Piedras have told me again and again that they don't believe in that stuff, that they're never going there again. When asked when they had gone for the last time, they characteristically replied, 'La semana pasada. Pero no vuelvo mas.'

These barmaids would have all have classified themselves as 'Black'; perhaps no one would so classify all of them. They, and a great deal of other data, bring up the most intriguing possibility of them all – the influence of Blacks on whites in the New World. As in the case of dialects,[17] it seems unavoidable – despite bitter denials – that there has been such influence, in the American South as elsewhere. One of Hyatt's informants observed, 'Well, the majority is colored people, but we got right smart of white – right smart of them.'[18] There has hardly begun to be any investigation of the situation in which, for a given area or activity, the Blacks constituted the majority.[19] But the postponing of such investigations has drawn a veil across what may be the most important aspects of the history of our folk culture.[20]

As elsewhere, Puerto Rican studies have been carried out by those who simply assume that no African influence on the white population has been possible. The folk say 'El que no tiene Dinga tiene Mandingo', but scholars debate whether there has been any African influence. They usually conclude that there has been very little.[21]

The study of Black names has thus suffered from an incredible ignorance of the very basis of Black culture. As pointed out many times, Black English was not recognized by dialectologists because they were so deeply involved in the Proto-Indo-European reconstructive tradition that they were incapable of recognizing the type of language variation which was going on all around them. The kind of people who sampled Black-white 'cultural' differences by eliciting words for a kind of pastry made with corn meal and the name for the vehicle to which a mule could be hitched for plowing also sampled onomastic patterns by looking at the official designations for places.[22] It is no wonder that they found no Black traditions; but, in dialect as in onomastics, their 'conclusions' prove nothing.[23]

Notes

NOTES TO 'INTRODUCTION: THE PROBLEM OF BLACK NAMES'

1. For such a claim about the Black English Vernacular, see Lawrence Davis, 'Dialect Research: Mythology vs. Reality', *Orbis* XVIII (1969): 332–337. 'Existence' of the Black English Vernacular is called into question here, not on complex epistemological grounds, but in a context in which the 'reality' of other dialects and language varieties is unquestioningly assumed. For questioning of the existence of West African vehicle names, in some areas, see Chapter 3, p. 6.
2. An instructive example can be found in the progress of the work by William Labov. In Labov, Cohen, Robins (1965:51), he asserted that *they book, they-selves* must be the result of phonological rules, since 'we have no parallel evidence for *I book, she book,* or *we book'*. With the possible exception of the first, however, these are extremely familiar in the related West Indian island varieties.
   Labov, Cohen, Robins, and Lewis (1968, Vol. I) give many examples of structures like those denied in 1965 – with, unfortunately, no apparatus for calling attention to the change.
   Likewise, Labov et al., 1965, minimized the grammatical differences and attributed the differences to phonological rules. Labov et al., 1968, tackled the problem of 'an underlying Creole grammar' (I: Chapter 1, 1.1.3) and rejected that theory, as expressed in the works of Stewart (1967). By implication, they also rejected the Creole origins theory (Stewart 1967, 1968; Dillard 1972). On the other hand, Labov, 'Negative Attraction and Negative Concord in English Grammar,' *Language* XLVIII (1972): 713–818 asserts, in a footnote, the truth of the Creolist hypothesis.
   Labov, *Language in the Inner City*, 1972, now asserts that *been* in certain preverbal contexts (*I been know your name, I been own one of these*) 'is normally not understood at all by speakers of other dialects' (p. 54). In accepting the Creole origin hypothesis and acknowledging at least some grammatical difference between the two varieties, Labov would seem to have almost completely reversed his earlier position. As is usual in such cases, however, no published acknowledgement of that reversal has been given.
3. For discussion of this question, see Frank Anshen, 'Some Statistical Bases for the Existence of Black English', *Florida FL Reporter*, Spring/Fall, 1972: 19–20.

4. Cf. especially the statement by Norman Whitten, quoted extensively below.
5. Stanley M. Elkins, *Slavery, A Problem in American Institutional and Intellectual Life*, 1965, presents the classical example, comparing the plantation slave camps to Nazi concentration camps. See Genovese 1974, Wood 1974, and Fogel and Ingerman 1974, for the inevitable reaction and putting into perspective of such overstatements. It must be obvious, even from the truism that Nazis were aiming at the reduction of the Jewish population whereas slaveowners were aiming for the increase of the slave population, that opportunities for a kind of social adjustment were much greater for the enslaved Black West Africans than for the interned Jewish people.
6. *Atlantic Monthly* LXVII (January, 1891): 143–144. Reprinted in Bruce Jackson (ed.), *The Negro and his Folklore in Nineteenth-Century Periodicals*, 1967.
7. His *Myth of the Negro Past*, originally published in 1941, is of course the best-known such statement. Other important statements were 'The Negro in the New World: The Statement of a Problem', *American Anthropologist* 32 (1930): 145–155; 'Problem, Method and Theory in Afroamerican Studies', *Afroamerica* I (1–2): 5–24. See also Herskovits and Herskovits (1936).
8. McDavid, 'Historical, Regional, and Social Variation', *Journal of English Linguistics* I (1967): 25–40 attempted to trace the Ø ending of the third person singular, present indicative verb form as used by Black speakers to East Anglian dialect. See my attack on that position in 'Nonstandard Negro Dialects – Convergence or Divergence?', *Florida FL Reporter* VI (1968): 9–10, 12, reprinted in Whitten and Szwed (eds.), *Afro-American Anthropology*. McDavid's position in the 1967 article, although rather obviously absurd when considered by itself, follows quite naturally from the preconceptions and working methods of dialect geography. (On the distortions inherent in those preconceptions and working methods, see Glenna Ruth Pickford, 'American Linguistic Geography: A Sociological Appraisal', *Word*, 1956.)
    Since I believe that the heavy dependence upon place name studies for general culture history has played an important part in setting up the kind of preconceptions within which the dialect geographers work, and since I believe that the principles and findings of dialect geography are now a hindrance to serious investigation, I have aimed this book essentially at a demonstration of how non-geographic onomastic traditions may support a very different picture. For more criticism of the geographic Atlas procedures, see my 'Lay My Isogloss Bundle Down: The Contribution of Black English to American Dialectology', *Linguistics* 119 (1974): 5–14.
9. Norman Whitten, 'Contemporary Patterns of Malign Occultism Among Negroes in North Carolina', in Dundes (ed.), *Mother Wit from the Laughing Barrel*, p. 415.
10. *Ibid.*, p. 415.
11. *Ibid.*, p. 416
12. For a collection of articles having this orientation, see Williamson and Burke (eds.), *A Various Language*, 1971. My review is in *Caribbean Studies* IV (1973): 76–91.
13. An extreme example of the loss of any real sense of the place of origin of the Black population of the United States can be seen in the term *Libyan* in Harriet Beecher Stowe's article 'Sojourner Truth: The Libyan Sibyl', *Atlantic Monthly*, 1863. The use of *Ethiopian* for anything pertaining to Africa is perhaps equally symptomatic, although perhaps not quite so indicative of

historical irresponsibility. Cf. Sandoval, *De Instauranda Aethiopium Salute*, 1627.

14. Robert B. Lepage, 'An Historical Introduction to Jamaican Creole', Part I of LePage and DeCamp, *Creole Studies I: Jamaican Creole* (London, 1960) makes a valiant attempt to establish some kind of dominance of Gold Coast ('Cormantin') slaves in Jamaica – because of the supposed preponderance of Twi loanwords in Jamaican Africanisms. He concludes, however, '. . . despite the preference shown in Jamaica for Gold Coast slaves, these could at no time have constituted the major part of slave imports' (p. 75).

15. Perhaps the most instructive insight into the relationship of dialect geography and internal reconstruction comes from reading Bloomfield's *Language* (1933), Chapter 18 and the first paragraph of Chapter 19. The last sentence in that paragraph – by a writer who was always a master of concise statement – reveals a great deal about the preconceptions of scholars who have supposedly been working on dialect variation in languages like present-day English. Bloomfield, who reacted favorably to dialect geography while clearly recognizing that its primary function was as a supplement to internal reconstruction, hypothesized 'density of communication' as the primary factor in dialect influence – and, therefore, presumably in linguistic change. A great many modern studies, the most significant of which is in my opinion John Gumperz, 'Dialect and Social Stratification' (*American Anthropologist*, 1958), have challenged that explanation. To a great extent, Bloomfield's theoretical orientation reflected early Behaviorism (or, as he would have put it, Physicalism). The whole recent anti-behaviorist reaction of Chomsky and his followers (especially *Language and Mind*, 1968) is counter to this orientation. For a collection with a very different orientation, see Charles-James N. Bailey and Roger W. Shuy (eds.), *New Ways of Analyzing Variation in English*, Georgetown University Press, 1973.

16. Richard Price (ed.), *Maroon Societies; Rebel Communities in the Americas*, Garden City, New York, 1973, p. 28. The other works of Price (see Bibliography for a small partial list) have been very important for the problem of examining deep-level and surface relationships in Afro-American culture.

17. See William R. Bascom, 'Acculturation Among the Gullah Negroes', *American Anthropologist*, 1941; Samuel C. Adams, Jr., 'The Acculturation of the Delta Negro', *Social Forces* 26 (1947): 202–205; and Herskovits, *The New World Negro*, 1966, especially p. 23.

18. The statement below, while perhaps an extreme example, is not too unrepresentative of the orientation of thoughtless place-name researchers:

    The English colonist, landing in the New World, was confronted with a virtually nameless landscape (Janet H. Gritzner, 'Culture and Process on the Eastern Shore', *Names* 20 (1974): 239).

    In the same article, Gritzner quotes with approval Wilbur Zelinsky's statement ('Some Problems in the Distribution of Generic Terms in the Place Names of the Northeastern United States', *Annals of the Association of American Geographers*, 1969, p. 319) and an article by E. Joan Wilson ('Naming of the Land of the Arkansas Ozarks', *Annals of the Association of American Geographers*, 1969, pp. 240–251) which stress the importance of place names for cultural history without considering other naming patterns.

19. C-J. N. Bailey, 'Review of Dillard, *Black English*', *Foundations of Language* 11 (1974), p. 302.

20. DeCamp, 'Cart Names in Jamaica', 1960, p. 17.
21. See Cassidy, *Jamaica Talk*, 1961.
22. The usual fanciful etymology was given to me by informants in Christian-sted, St. Croix: There was a wealthy man who had a favorite daughter named Judith. For her birthday (or some other such occasion) he offered her her 'fancy'. She 'fancied' the estate. Although the name appears on the maps as *Judith's Fancy*, a signpost near the estate as the more Creole *Judith Fancy* (with possession by juxtaposition).
23. Horace Sutton, column in *Chicago Tribune*, 1971.
24. *Ibid.*
25. The really fascinating suggestions, such as the one concerning the *Bogue* Islands of Montego Bay in Cassidy, *Jamaica Talk*, 1961, pp. 119–120, are never followed up. Cassidy cites the *Dictionary of Americanisms*, which in turn cites Spanish *boca* (from 1832) and *bogue* (also from 1832). The DA traces the latter 'through American French to Choctaw *bok*, *bouk*, reduced forms of *bayuk*, from which comes the Louisiana *bayou*'. The whole re-lationship recalls *lagniappe*, which presumably goes back to Quechua *ñapa* and then to Louisiana through French. In Louisiana, it is often regarded as one of the more reliable indices of the local area dialect. It is quite notable, however, that the first citation in the DA credits the term to 'our Creole Negroes'. Although apparently common enough in Jamaica to warrant in-clusion in Cassidy and LePage, *Dictionary of Jamaicanisms* (1968), the term is also widely current in the Caribbean – including (as *la ñapa*) Puerto Rico. The major point here, which seems to have been overlooked completely by the dialect geographers, is that a great deal of interaction between slaves from West Africa and American Indians had important consequences for the language history of North America. See my *Black English* (1972), Chapter IV, and *All-American English* (1975), Chapters III and IV.
26. DeCamp (1960: 18).
27. Fairclough (1960: 79): 'White Baptist congregations in New Orleans are distinguished today, as they were in 1941, by a definite predilection for secular names, and particularly for secular place names'. As Fairclough himself is careful to establish, church names outside New Orleans follow the same pattern. Such place names as he observes in the Black churches, on the other hand, are Biblical place names: Mount Ararat, Mount Carmel, Mount Zion, Zion Hill, Beulah Land.
28. This is, of course, a beautiful example of one of the best-known structures of the Creole languages – non-redundant pluralization. The same child would write *the ponies* (or, maybe, *ponys*) but Creole grammar does not demand a plural marker on the noun when a numeral (or other clear pluralizer) precedes the noun. Although the girl, like most such students, was writing in Standard English, Creole grammar typically crept in from time to time. It is to be hoped that no reader is so pedantic as to find any-thing significant about the spelling *to*.
29. For personal names and for ship names, especially, comparison to such non-traditional patterns as the names of pirates and pirate ships might turn out to be very fruitful. P. K. Kemp and Christopher Lloyd, *The Brethren of the Coast*, give examples of Pirate nicknames like

Bâbord-Amure	Brise-Goulets
Pass-Partout	l'Hallebarde
Vent-en-Panne	Borgne-Fesse

See also John Esquemeling, *The Buccaniers of America* (1684). An attempt to cope with the maritime influence on early American English is made in Dillard, *All-American English* (1975). Even the platitude that Black slaves were brought over from West Africa on ships would seem to establish the importance of maritime traditions in Black history, if it were not otherwise known that Blacks were often employed in ship's crews (see Hugh Crow 1791). A maritime or pirate tradition, while it might be in some sense more 'European' than West African, would hardly be European in the sense in which the term is used in linguistic treatments of New World populations.

NOTES TO CHAPTER 1: 'PERSONAL NAMES'

1. For some material concerning the Ras Tafarians and their aspirations with regard to Ethiopia, see Donald Hogg, 'Statement of a Ras Tafari Leader', *Caribbean Studies* 6 (1) (April, 1966): 37–38.
2. In their simplest form, the day names consisted of

	Male	*Female*
Sunday	Quashee	Quasheba
Monday	Cudjo	Juba
Tuesday	Cubbenah	Beneba
Wednesday	Kwaco, Quaco	Cuba
Thursday	Quao	Abba
Friday	Cuffee, Cuffy	Pheba, Phibbi
Saturday	Quame, Kwame	Mimba

There were many variants, as for example *Cuff* for *Cuffee*, in both West Africa and the New World. Turner (1949: 43) lists the correspondence between Fante Aba and Twi Ya 'name given a girl born on Thursday'.
3. Genovese (1974: 449) writes that 'African names steadily receded after the turn of the nineteenth century, as a review of the slave names that appear in court records show, but they never wholly disappeared'. He cites the case of ex-slave Martin Jackson, of Texas:

> One of my grandfathers in Africa was called Jeaceo, and so I decided to be Jackson (quoted from Yetman [ed.], *Life Under the 'Peculiar Institution'*, 1970, p. 175).

Wood (1974: 184–185) cites the 'long-term social pressures which caused many personal names to disappear, at least from public use', notes the same essential process where 'non-English-speaking groups have imported names', and compares the pejoration of the day names in Jamaica as treated by DeCamp (1967). Something of the same thing obviously happened in the United States. In Nathaniel Beverly Tucker's *Partisan Leader* (1836), the common-noun use of *a cuffee* may be observed, in a context in which the term is far from flattering. See also Dillard (1972: 130) on Sambo.
4. As DeCamp shows, Cuffee has come to mean 'a simpleton; a bully; a left-handed man'. Perhaps even more significant is what has happened to the day names for females. Quasheba means 'a foolish, ne'er-do-well woman; a prostitute', and the other names have striking tendencies to acquire connotations of sexual promiscuity. Cassidy (1961: 157) cites Moreton's couplet

When pepper-pot and wine his blood alarms,
He takes a quashiba into his arms.

(*His*, of course, refers to the white master.)

The day names were familiar in the United States and in England (see Hans Nathan, *Dan Emmett and the Rise of Early Negro Minstrelsy*, 1962, Chapter 2).

The low state into which the day names had fallen by the time of the Civil War is in no way inconsistent with the pride taken in them by those who participated in the early slave revolts. Rather, the common factor (to Black revolutionaries and to low status Blacks) was resistance to acculturation.

5. *Decreolization* refers to the process by which a Creole language changes in the direction of a 'standard' variety of a language with which it shares a certain amount of the lexicon. See Stewart (1968).

6. See Jan Voorhoeve, 'Historical and Linguistic Evidence in Favour of the Relexification Theory in the Formation of Creoles', *Language in Society* 2 (1) (April, 1973): 133–146. Voorhoeve's use of different terms, like *partly relexified* is of no immediate importance here.

7. P. Grade, 'Das Neger-English an der Westküste von Afrika', *Anglia* XIV (1892): 362–393, presents a Pidgin English dialogue between 'ein Kuneger, Friday' and another African.

8. The example was given to me by my wife, Margie I. Dillard.

9. See Gilbert Schneider, *First Steps in Wes-Kos*, 1963, pp. 35, 77.

10. Alan Dundes (ed.), *Mother Wit from the Laughing Barrel*, 1973, p. 159.

11. *Ibid.*

12. Milford A. Jeremiah, *The Linguistic Relatedness of Black English and Antiguan Creole*, unpublished dissertation (Brown University), 1975.

13. Bryan Edwards, 'Observations on the Disposition, Character, Manners, and Habits of Life of the Maroon Negroes of the Island of Jamaica . . .', in *The History . . . of the West Indies*, London, 1807, I, pp. 537–545.

14. Judith Farmer, unpublished report for Sociolinguistics seminar, Georgetown University, 1967.

15. See Harriet Beecher Stowe, 'Sojourner Truth, the Libyan Sibyl', *Atlantic Monthly*, 1863: 473–481, and Arthur Huff Fauset, *Sojourner Truth – God's Faithful Pilgrim*, University of North Carolina Press, 1938.

16. For an enlightening approach in terms of broader language matters, see David Dalby, 'The African Element in American English', in Thomas Kochman (ed.), *Rappin' and Stylin' Out: Communication in Urban Black America*, University of Illinois Press, 1972. Dalby points out that expressions like *bad-mouth* 'slander, abuse, gossip', *be with it* 'to be in fashion', *big eye* 'greedy' correspond to West African languages which combine the same words (translated) into the same meaning. It is true (and irrelevant) that none of the words cited is etymologically African. White Americans have the usual rationalizations of these phrases, including the 'explanation' that *big eye* refers to a situation involving 'big I and little you (u)'. It is probable that there is not a single Africanism in any Pidgin, Creole, or partly decreolized variety for which some such rationalization has not been offered. A collection of them could make up an amusing contribution to the folklore of language.

17. Wherever possible, the names are presented in ordinary English orthography rather than in Schneider's phonemic transcription. There is West African precedent for a Europeanizing orthography in the column 'King for Toly' in *Le Courrier Sportif*, published in Doula, Cameroun, for a period around 1965.

18. This intensification by reduplication is very common in Caribbean Creoles. See F. G. Cassidy, 'Iteration as a Word-forming Device in Jamaican Folk Speech', *American Speech* XXXII (1957): 49–53. For the same device in Cameroonian Pidgin, see Schneider, *First Steps in Wes-Kos*, p. 7.
19. There is, of course, other such documentation. William A. Stewart cites the following from John Atkins, *A Voyage to Guinea, Brazil, and the West Indies*, London, 1735:

> They give Names to their Children, mostly by the days of the Week born on, *Quashee, Yeday, Cuujo*, that is, *Sunday, Monday, Tuesday*, &c. and at Manhood, change it to something expressive of their Disposition; *Aquerro Occu, Yocatee, Tittwee*, like a *Parrot, Lion, Wolf*, &c. The same they do by white Men, imposing a Name of their own chusing (pp. 99–100).

Stewart's paper, 'Acculturative Processes and the Language of the American Negro', is to appear in William W. Gage (ed.), *Language in its Social Setting*, forthcoming.

20. *The Myth of the Negro Past*, Beacon Edition, 1958, p. 193. Herskovits quotes Botume on how ' "Cornhouse" yesterday was "Primus" today. That "Quash" was Bryan'. Any investigator into Afro-American language and culture soon realizes that his task consists largely of expanding Herskovits's outlines and confirming his insights.
21. *Mother Wit from the Laughing Barrel*, p. 169.
22. *Ibid.*, p. 167.
23. Frank E. Manning, 'Nicknames and Number Plates in the British West Indies', *Journal of American Folklore* 87 (1974): 123–132. Other nicknames listed by Manning are 'DA', 'Hungry', 'Smock', 'Smokey', 'Bouncer', 'Stagolee', 'Tuppence', 'Peacemaker', and 'Comical World'. He further points out that the Bermuda telephone directory actually contains many such nicknames: 'Nappy', 'Centipede', 'Snooks', 'Squeaky', 'Captain Tired', and 'hundreds of other sobriquets', ten more of which are listed. Manning points out that women use such nicknames much less frequently than men – which would, of course, support the theory of origin in something like the Pidgin English work names.
24. *New York Post*, January 11, 1975, p. 21.
25. See note 18.
26. Henry A. Kiner, 'Old Corn Meal: A Forgotten Urban Negro Folksinger', *Journal of American Folklore* 75 (1962): 29–34.
27. Alan Lomax, *Mister Jelly Roll*, New York, 1950, pp. 44–45.
28. *Ibid.*, p. 42.
29. *Ibid.*, p. 136.
30. *Jelly Roll* is, like *piece of bread*, etc., one of the many allusions to sexual intercourse phrased in terms of pastry. Harold Courlander, *Negro Folk Music, U.S.A.*, p. 129, compares 'Custard Pie Blues' as an example of 'this kind of Metaphor'. Although he does not directly refer to the 'Jelly Roll Blues', he must have assumed that any interested reader would be familiar with that song. The line 'Ain't gonna give nobody none of my jelly roll' obviously refers, at one level, to unwillingness to share a girl friend's favors. Lomax, *op. cit.*, p. 136, refers to 'a folk simile of sexual reference which antedates Morton's rechristening'. Dalby, 'The African Element in American English', pp. 181–182, cites Mandingo *jeli* 'minstrel', 'often gaining popularity

with women through his skill in the use of words and music'. There is probably still more to this allusion. In Caribbean English, *jelly* refers to the meat of the not quite ripe coconut, which is clear-colored and in a state between liquid and solid; in short, it looks like nothing more than semen. A *jelly roll*, at one level of meaning, is a roll ('in the hay') which produces jelly – semen. There is probably still another level. Like *cake* in blues terminology, *jelly roll* is a 'good piece', from a young and attractive woman who cooperates and is not like the other type of woman who has 'cornbread' – perhaps, in some cases, 'Cornbread for her husband – biscuits for her backdoor man'.

Whether or not Jelly Roll Morton was the first in jazz to utilize this metaphor, he was certainly not the last. As Dalby also points out, other musicians (Jelly Williams and Jelly Thompson) used a similar nickname. In blues lyrics, the metaphor is familiar in

> Jelly, jelly, jelly, jelly stays on my mind;
> Jelly roll killed my pappy; it drove my mammy stone blind

and perhaps even more so in Ida Cox's 'Fogyism', where an unfaithful man is characterized in the terms 'he's got someone else baking his jelly roll'.

31. Dalby, *op. cit.*, cites Mandingo *jasi*, Temne *yas*. He asserts that the basic verbal sense is 'to speed up, excite, exaggerate, act in an unrestrained or extreme way' and that the term is 'hence applied to copulation, frenzied dancing, fast-tempo music, exaggerated talk, gaudy patterns and colors, excessive pleasure-seeking, etc.'. Again, titles like 'Jazz Me Blues' play on the sexual sense of the word.

32. See Herskovits, 'What Has Africa Given America?' *The New World Negro*, 1966, p. 172.

33. See, for example, Langston Hughes and Milton Meltzner, *Black Magic, A Pictorial History of the Negro in American Entertainment*, 1967, *passim*, and Richard Middleton, *Pop Music and the Blues*, London, 1972.

34. Cf. Marshall Stearns and Jean Stearns, 'Frontiers of Humor: American Vernacular Dance', *Southern Folklore Quarterly* 30 (1966): 227–235, reprinted in Dundes (ed.), *Mother Wit from the Laughing Barrel*.

35. *Mother Wit from the Laughing Barrel*, p. 617.

36. *Ibid.*, p. 167.

37. In mere outlandishness, of course, names of the early Puritans (like the celebrated Praise God Barebones) could top these Black names. Otherwise, however, there is little similarity. Anyone should be able to distinguish a lot of Black nicknames from a list of Puritan names. Puckett (1937) discusses the influence of Puritan names like Fortune, Providence, Comfort, Piety, and Prudence on the slave population.

38. Sources include Hughes and Meltzner, 1967; Hugues Panassie and Madeleine Gautier, *Guide to Jazz*, 1956; LeRoi Jones, *Blues People*; Marshall Stearns, *The Story of Jazz*; Frederic Ramsey, Jr., and Charles Edward Smith, *Jazzmen*; Gunther Schuller, *Early Jazz*; Marshall and Jean Stearns, *Jazz Dance*; Harold Courlander, *Negro Folk Music, U.S.A.*; Robert George Reisner, *The Jazz Titans*; Rudi Blesh and Harriet Janis, *They All Played Ragtime*; Nat Shapiro and Nat Hentoff, *Jazz Makers*; Nat Hentoff and Albert McCarthy, *Jazz*; Martin Williams, *Jazz Panorama*; Martin T. Williams (ed.), *The Art of Jazz*; Wilfrid Mellers, *Music in a New Found Land; Themes and Developments in the History of American Music*; Howard W. Odum

and Guy B. Johnson, *Negro Workaday Songs*; David Ewen, *The Life and Death of Tin Pin Alley*; and numerous articles in journals like the *Journal of American Folklore*. Some of them were also taken from the backs of record jackets and from advertisements in newspapers, etc. Some preference was given to early sources, since the interest of this research is primarily historical.

39. Dalby (1972:177) lists *bad-eye* 'threatening, hateful glance' and compares Mandingo *nye-jugu* 'hateful glance', literally 'bad-eye'.
40. Cf. Dalby on *big eye* 'greedy'. None of the sources, however, assert that this nickname had that significance.
41. Ramsay and Smith, *Jazzmen*, p. 198.
42. Note, however, that only 'Slew-foot Pete' represents an attribute, either actual or hoped for.
43. Statements about the influence of the Black 'mammy' on the white children are very familiar to those who have studied the plantation literature. See Dillard, *Black English* (1972: 198–207) and Genovese, *Roll, Jordan, Roll* (1974: 356–361).
   Serious historical students must be prepared, however, to reinterpret such statements in terms of the greater likelihood that peer group relationships (however transitory) with Black children would have been much more effective than child-adult relationships. For a lucid statement of the linguistic importance of the peer group, see Labov 1972, pp. 53–55. That the importance of the peer-group relationship is slowly penetrating the consciousness even of dialect geographers is evident from Underwood (1974).
44. Quoted in Stewart (forthcoming). Although it seldom shows up in his writings, Stewart's public lectures have always contained beautiful examples of how Blacks and whites of the same region may have very different characteristic behavioral (especially kinesic) patterns. His articles, on the other hand, have always dealt almost exclusively with linguistic differences. It is noteworthy that an article by Stewart has also some of the most convincing evidence of Black influence on white behavioral patterns. His work is therefore perhaps the most important since that of Herskovits in refuting the traditional paradigm that Black and white behavioral patterns of a given region must be identical because the Blacks learned them all from whites. (A very moderately more sophisticated version of that paradigm allows for Black-white differences, *at the present time, because* of differential migration patterns. Since writers on such patterns are often embarrassed to acknowledge even the existence of slavery, they quite often miss the point completely: 'Different migration patterns' occurred from the beginning of Black-white relationships in the New World, not just in some conveniently demarcated period like that between World War I or World War II and the present.)

NOTES TO CHAPTER 2: 'JAZZ, BLUES, AND ROCK BANDS AND THEIR TITLES'

1. This is a commonplace of jazz history. See, however, Charles Edward Smith, 'New Orleans and Traditions in Jazz', in Hentoff and McCarthy (eds.), *Jazz*.
2. Frederic Ramsay, Jr., and Charles Edward Smith, *Jazzmen*, pp. 16–17.
3. *Ibid.*
4. *Ibid.*
5. *Ibid.* Hughes and Meltzner (1967) cite examples of elaborate names used by

other Black entertainment groups, going back as far as Callender's Consolidated Spectacular Colored Minstrels (1882).

6. Margie Ivey Dillard, a resident of the area from 1945–1949, and Charles Hayes, born and reared in Southern Louisiana. Both of these have given valuable information and interesting discussions of the matters under consideration here.
7. See Chapter 1, note 32.
8. Mezzrow, *Really the Blues, passim.*
9. See Tony Russell, *Blacks, Whites, and the Blues,* New York, 1970.
10. Before that, Black music had influenced the 'hillbilly' tradition. See John Cohen, 'The Folk Music Interchange: Negro and White', *Sing Out:* Dec. 1964 – Jan. 1965.
11. Harold Courlander, *Negro Folk Music, U.S.A.,* p. 35.
12. Mack McCormack, 'Lightnin' Hopkins: Blues', in Martin Williams (ed.), *Jazz Panorama,* writes of 'rock and roll: a form of the blues designed by sound engineers for the thump and screech acoustics of a juke box'. Slonimsky, somewhat more tolerant, still asserts that 'the weaker rhythms of country music overflowed the syncopation of classical jazz and reduced the aggressive asymmetry of the urban product to the monotony of an even beat in square time'.
13. Jeff Greenfield, 'They Changed Rock, Which Changed the Culture, Which Changed Us', *New York Times Magazine,* February 16, 1975, writes that the Beatles 'grew up as children of the first generation of rock 'n' roll, listening to and imitating the music of Little Richard, Larry Williams, Chuck Berry, Elvis Presley, and the later, more sophisticated sounds of the Shirelles and the Miracles' (p. 37). One can, I believe trust such factual information from a writer like Greenfield without sharing his feeling that a 'culture' is so easily changed.
14. The tracing of the *Moondog* element in the early name to the Broadway street musician is my own, insofar as I know, since I can find no reference to it in any readily available source. References to that musician used to be quite common in the column which Walter Winchell wrote for the old *New York Daily Mirror,* particularly in those rather frequent columns in which Winchell essayed a kind of 'Panorama of Broadway' in a highly sentimental vein. Slonimsky describes the eventual name The Beatles as an 'inspired sobriquet' (p. 1145) and calls it 'a palimpsest of Beat and Beetles' (p. 1846). This may be the only occasion on which the word *palimpsest* has been used in connection with popular music.
15. Stearns and Stearns, *Jazz Dance,* report that 'the music was a throwback, or rather a dilution by white musicians of the kind of music recorded for the Negro market over the past fifty years'. They acknowledge, however, that 'For better or worse, rock-and-roll brought back popular dancing' (p. 1). Whatever the quality of the music, the very fact of the demand created among teenagers of many nations for electric guitars is a testimony to the influence of rock. Few, if any, other musical genres ever had such economic impact.
16. ' "I'm a Monkey", The Influence of the Black American Blues Argot on the Rolling Stones', *Journal of American Folklore* 86 (1973): 367–373.
17. *Ibid.,* p. 367.
18. See, for example, *Black English,* p. 240.
19. Hellman 1974: 371.
20. My teen-age rock enthusiast informants Dan Hinckley and Andy Lee of San

Juan, Puerto Rico, object that The Grateful Dead are a 'country rock' organization and Fifth Dimension a 'soul music' group. This does not seem to change the onomastic relationship. Neither, of course, does the relative artistic quality of any of these combos. My two young informants have not been in agreement on this matter, and have insisted (often scornfully) that one or another group is not worth including. There are probably some very good musical reasons for those objections. Whatever one's feeling about Rock and Roll, he would probably have to admit that Janis Jopin and Jimi Hendrix have a claim to performer status which they need not share with The Monkees. The latter are perhaps the most blatant of all the imitators of The Beatles. I can well remember, however, reading tributes to The Monkees from teen-age rock enthusiasts who wrote to the entertainment editor of the *Washington Post* in 1966–67. For purposes of inclusion in this list, the use of three electric guitars and drums outweighs such less tangible factors as musical creation.

21. *Funk*, meaning 'stench', is of course extremely familiar in Black ethnic slang. Mezzrow's Glossary is only one of very many sources for it. According to Jones, *Blues People:*

    The adjective *funky* which once meant to many Negroes merely a stink usually associated with sex), was used to qualify the music [hard bop] as meaningful (the word became fashionable and is now almost useless) (p. 219).

22. On *bad*, Dalby reports:

    In Black terms, it often means 'very good, extremely good'. It is an example of 'negative terms to describe positive extremes'.

    For such terms, and especially for the term *bad motherfucker*, see Ulf Hannerz, 'The Rhetoric of Soul', *Race* IX (1968): 453–465.

23. The comments are on the sleeve of the record called 'Stomps and Joys' (RCA Victor LPV-508).
24. Lomax, *Mr. Jelly Roll*, p. 112.
25. See Dalby 1972: 182–183.
26. Titles were taken from 'The Rural Blues', an RBF recording compiled and edited by Samuel Charters.
27. Taken from 'A Treasury of Field Recordings', 77-LA-12-3, compiled by Mack McCormick for 77 Records.
28. Taken from 'The Country Blues, Volume Two', compiled and edited by Samuel Charters for RBF.
29. Mezzrow, *Really the Blues*, Glossary. There appears to be no immediate evidence on the origin of this term. As always, discussion of vocabulary items in a 'Black English' or 'Black Names' context does not by any means imply that they are Africanisms in any direct sense, in spite of the impressive demonstrations by Dalby (1972) and others of the hidden African survivals in 'everyday' American vocabulary. (See especially Dalby on *O.K.*, and my discussion in support of that etymology in *All-American English: A History of American English*, 1975.) The following statement from Jones (1963: 23), although it makes somewhat more specific claims for direct African transmission than I would be willing to make, expresses the basic process extremely well:

    I do not mean actual surviving African words, but rather the African accent and the syntactical construction of certain West African dialects.

Since   Jones, immediately thereafter, cites Ashanti, he surely should have written *languages* rather than *dialects*.

NOTES TO CHAPTER 3: 'CHURCH NAMES'

1. See especially Charles Keil, *The Urban Blues*, 1966, for the close relationship between blues and rock and roll musicians and the church. Although traditional Black culture in the United States has consciously regarded blues and gospel music as antitheses (blues being of the devil, as gospel music relates one to God) the out-of-awareness traditions of performance have carried many of the devices of one over to the other. See John Szwed, 'Afro-American Musical Adaptation', in Whitten and Szwed (eds.), *Afro-American Anthropology: Contemporary Perspectives,* 1970.
2. See Alan Lomax, *Mr. Jelly Roll,* p. 244, for an extremely dramatic presentation of one musician's double religious allegiance.
3. *Blues People,* p. 74. From Trinidad, there is much better historical evidence than is available in the United States as to what the slave secret societies must have been like – and thus of what must have brought from Africa:

   . . . a number of organizations, inspired in part perhaps by recollection of the religious associations of the Guinea coast, were labeled 'secret societies' by prominent whites (Fraser 1826: 268–269) . . . Fraser wrote . . . 'the slaves . . . had formed themselves into "Convois" and "Regiments", each of which was known by its peculiar appelation. These were, for instance, the "Convois des Sans Peur" or "Dreadnaught Band"; the "Convoi de St. George"; the "Regiment Danois" or "Danish Regiment," which probably had been formed by slaves from St. Thomas or St. Croix; the "Regiment Macaque" or "Monkey Corps," and many other with titles more or less suggestive' (George Eaton Simpson, *The Shango Cult in Trinidad,* p. 12).

4. See Chapter 1, beginning, and note 1.
5. Lomax, *Mr. Jelly Roll,* p. 9.
6. *Gumbo Ya-Ya,* p. 309.
7. *Ibid.,* p. 311.
8. Herskovits 1967, I, 250–251.
9. Alfred Métraux, 'Cooperative Labor Groups in Haiti', in Michael Horowitz (ed.), *Peoples and Cultures of the Caribbean,* Natural History Press, 1971, pp. 318–339. Métraux discusses other labor groups, which are numerous in Haiti, but gives no other names. He does comment: 'When the Morne Rouge cooperative was established, titles were distributed with fantastic generosity.'
10. Note that the name, although in Creole, has been shifted toward French in the placement of the article before the noun.
11. 'The Acculturation of the Delta Negro', *Mother Wit from the Laughing Barrel,* p. 520.
12. Bascom, 'Acculturation Among the Gullah Negroes', *American Anthropologist,* 1941; reprinted in my *Perspectives on Black English*. The citation, in the latter collection, is on p. 283.
13. *Ibid.,* p. 285.
14. Fairclough 1960:84.
15. See *The Myth of the Negro Past*, 1958, and *The New World Negro,* 1966,

passim. In the latter collection, perhaps the clearest statement is in the article 'African Gods and Catholic Saints in New World Negro Belief', pp. 321–329.

16. Fairclough 1960: 83.
17. See the discussion of the descriptive terminology for the difference between Black and white naming patterns in the Introduction.
18. Fairclough 1960: 85.
19. *Ibid.*
20. Note that the somewhat synthetic Ethiopianism practiced among Negroes in the New World (see Chapter 1) is not unknown in West Africa.
21. Others listed by Parrinder are

United Native African Church   Aladura Church
Christ Apostolic Church (4)   Aladura Mission Church
Christ Apostolic Gospel Church   Aladura Apostolic Church

and four African language names.
22. This church had a Lady Bishop, Bishop Reed, as minister. She drove a car named Faith Chariot. Bishop Reed told me, in 1966, that there were four other such churches on the East Coast.
23. Nonstandard dialect elements (like *Move of God*, for *Mother...*) turn up fairly frequently. It seems obvious, however, that religious practices exercise a partial regularizing influence in language. Although preachers sometimes use *ain't* and other shibboleths of nonstandard usage to achieve solidarity with the congregation (the Reverend J. W. Evans of the Mt. Carmel Baptist Church, Los Angeles, whose sermons may be heard on Léshun Records 601-B, told graduate student Nancy McMillan of USC in the summer of 1968 that he consciously switched dialects), the more important transitions within the structure of the service are signaled through such metalinguistic devices as vocal rasp rather than by any more centrally linguistic devices. As a consequence, the preacher typically maintains a kind of authority over the congregation by using rather more standard English than they do. The vocal rasp is interesting in itself. Courlander (1963:23), who describes the quality as 'foggy, hoarse, rough, or sandy' has an interesting section on the preference for this type of voice over a 'smooth' or 'sweet' voice in Black communities in the United States, Haiti, and elsewhere.
24. Note that Parrinder (1953:126) traces the Nigerian Apostolic Faith group to direct contract with a group in Portland, Oregon. This name, however, comes not from Oregon at all but from the District of Columbia.
25. Note repetition of the element *Apostolic Faith*.
26. Note another repetition, as above. A study of the distribution of churches with this naming element might turn up some very interesting patterns.
27. These towns were chosen because they happen to be familiar to me personally and because I have recently conducted an investigation of the church names there. Examination of telephone directories in other towns in the American South (especially those printed in the days when it was permitted to differentiate *White Churches* from *Colored Churches*, denomination by denomination) reveal the same patterns in very many other places.
28. The linguistic controversy over Black American English seems directly parallel. Perhaps the issue was resolved only when it was finally decided that Black English has a 'remote present perfect' *been* + *Verb* which 'is not normally understood at all by speakers of other dialects' (Labov 1972:54).

It is interesting that Labov maintained for several years that Black English differed from other dialects only by phonological rules (primarily reductions) even though a description of *Been* + *Verb* had been published by Stewart (1964).
Other observers, like Loflin (all references) and Stewart (1964, 1968, 1968) found subtler differences in terms of co-occurrence potentialities with time adverbial modifiers (*inter alia*), even though the surface structure of the BEV verb phrase might not have been completely impossible in StE. Thus, BEV
he be dancing
can be masked, in the Herskovitsian sense, as a 'subjunctive'
StE If he be dancing . . .
despite the fact that the BEV form turns up in very many other environments. Only the isolation of environments like
He be dancing last Friday
really decides the issue, since StE
*If he be dancing last Friday
would hardly be suggested as a grammatical string.
The assertion that the church naming patterns are different from those of Standard English, even those found in white Baptist churches, rests on the same kind of 'subtler' evidence. We cannot point to lexical forms (except, trivially, *African, Ethiopian,* or the like) which occur in the Black church names and not in white church names. On the other hand, sensitive observers like Fairclough and Noreen had long been able to see something special about the Black ghetto naming practices. I believe – and I have written this book largely for the purpose of trying to support that belief – that the evidence of naming patterns gives some justification to those who, like Stewart (1964, 1967, 1968, etc.), Loflin (all references), and Fickett (1970) recognize the autonomy of Black English.
That the linguists who have written of Black English as a valid system because of its different syntactic patterns have not been abusing the tradition of studies in language variation is carefully pointed out by Preston (1972):

> The more difficult notion to deal with in Davis's charges that various new methods of data analysis will not allow us to call Black English a dialect is his final contention that Black English differs 'quantitatively' but not 'qualitatively' from White English. ... Unfortunately, this reasoning would not only play havoc with traditional statements about dialect but also force us to revise all notions of historical linguistics (pp. 15–16).

If, however, *been* in *been know* is allowed to be 'qualitatively' different from (e.g.) *have been knowing* (see discussion in preceding paragraphs), then the entire objection posed by Davis (1969) proves to be vacuous.
Preston's arguments about the validity of 'quantitative' differences for dialect differentiation remain important, however, for such matters as the church names. If the 'qualitative' reactions of observers like Fairclough – however poorly they may be substantiated in purely formal terms – can be supported by formal demonstrations such as the difference between right- and left-branching patterns, then it would seem to make no difference whether any significant portion of the vocabulary utilized in the church names is different.

NOTES TO CHAPTER 4: 'VEHICLE NAMES'

1. Compare Trus-me-God as a Gullah designation for a canoe. See below, note 40 and text.
2. Compare Save Journey, the bus name which is also the title for a radio program (episodic comedy) in Nigeria. The driver of the bus is Shakey Shakey (Shakespeare).
3. This name was given to me orally by Ian F. Hancock, who did not report the spelling used. The usual practice in such names is to use a spelling very close to that of Standard English: *talk*, not *tok* or something similar. (See below, note 4.) *Hear* would, however, be too unlike the actual pronunciation – with initial palatalized glide and final enclitic vowel – to be an acceptable spelling.
4. As in representing the name from Sierra Leone (see note 3), I have used an approximate Standard English spelling rather than Schneider's phonemic transcriptions. This is what I actually observed in the mammy wagon names of the West Cameroon, although deviations both in orthography and phonology often marked the influence of Pidgin English. Where, however, Schneider has /dey/ I have used *Dey* rather than the absurdly unpidgin-like *There* or *Dere*. (The latter renderings of Standard English are also wildly inaccurate as a suggestion of the grammar of the pidgin word.) The name God Dey (Schneider's /got dey/) 'means' *God is there*, but to use either that phrase or something like *God There* would be to misrepresent the actual mammy wagon name entirely. Compare the other West Cameroonian, Nigerian, and Ghanian names (below) for an indication of the orthographic practices of the namers themselves.
5. Man is not God. The copula structure of Pidgin English demands *be* between Noun Subject and Noun Complement. Compare *Pam Be Civil* from the early Jamaican materials, cited below.
6. These words are regularly written on the mammy wagons with ordinary *c*, without the cedilla. Here, as elsewhere, the aim is to represent the names as they were, not to produce 'correct' French.
7. Others in my collection, not discussed in the body of the text, are

Avili Car	Alla Karim
(Back: Au Revoir Avili)	(Back: Gentil Car)
Rien N'Est Total Dans la Vie	L'Ombre du Plaisir
(Back: Bon Voyage)	(Back: Toujours a l'Heure)
Toujours Rapide	Dieu Roi de Ma Souffrance
(Back: Toujours Rapide)	Rayon Matinal
Dizangue Car	On Ne Sait Jamais
(Back: Bonne Route)	Chacun Pour Soi
Ami des Jeunes	Nkam Car
(Back: Ami des Jeunes)	Vie Routiere du Cameroun
Federal de NDE	(Back: Exception)
(Back: Federal de NDE)	De La Salle
Providence Car	Vie Tranquille
(Back: Espoir de L'Etat)	Dieu Pour Tous
Bon Marche	Famille Car
(Back: La Main dans La Main)	La Fête du Mouton
Ne T'Empresse Pas	Ne T'Impresse Pas
(Back: Allons Doucement)	L'Ami Du Progress

Cameroun Federal Car
Sans Peur – Sans Reproche
Papa Niko
Aimons-Nous Car
Cheri Car
L'Espoir
Regulier du Cameroun
Rapide de l'Ouest
No Credit Today

Regulier Bamileke
(Back: L'Ami Du Progress)
Aimez Son Prochain Comme Soi
Meme
Dieu Nous Aime
On Ne Sait Pas
(Back: Tout Depend de Dieu)
Gentil Car Cha! Cha

As has been asserted above, almost any observer who visits West Africa must have noted many such names. John Gunther's *Inside Africa* (1953) comments on the names in Ibadan, Nigeria:

> Most 'mammy wagons' have slogans painted on them, like 'God Is Good' or 'We Believe in the United Africa Company' (p. 761).

And of Accra, Gold Coast:

> The legends on the trucks and lorries are even more fancifully bizarre than those in Nigeria. I saw God's Time Is the Best, Safety First with God, Proud Old Man, All the World's a Stage (on a cinema van), See Before You Say, My Happiness, Abomination Has No Remedy, and God The Killer (p. 832).

8. Neither my own collection nor any statement I have been able to get from informants includes anything from Papiamentu-speaking islands. Specifically, Paul Baum, of the Colegio Universitario del Sagrado Corazon, Hato Rey, Puerto Rico, who did a dissertation on Papiamentu at the University of Puerto Rico and who did extensive field work on Curaçao, was unable to recall seeing any such names in the 'ABC' islands. Since Baum collected the St. Kitts names treated later, he had at least an *ex post facto* awareness of what might have been there to be found. As will be evident in the examples given, mixing of languages and occurrence of nonstandard forms in individual languages are regular parts of this onomastic process.

9. This is a familiar idea – to Afro-Caribbeanists at least – and probably needs no documentation. Erika Bourguignon, 'Ritual Dissociation and Possession Belief in Caribbean Negro Religion' (in Whitten and Szwed, 1970) begins an examination of African survivals with 'Haiti and its Cognate Societies' and writes of the 'Afro-Haitian pattern'. Many others have, of course, made equivalent statements.

10. In Foumban, capital of the Moslem Bamoun tribe in the Cameroun, I was surrounded by chauffeurs when I tried to copy down the many names on buses in a parking lot. The drivers were highly suspicious, and only some earnest explanation got me off with a whole skin and an incomplete list. In Guadeloupe, a policeman stopped me for questioning but finally decided (without being told by me) that I was an inspector for the Renault company (which manufactures the minibuses which are used there). A passerby – in Haiti! – asked me if I were a member of the police. In Yaoundé, both Camerounians and Europeans carefully explained to me that such names were found only in the West Cameroon. Nevertheless, I collected at least half of the French-language names presented here in Yaoundé. Such reluctance to divulge the actual state of an old-fashioned culture trait is, of course, commonplace among informants in all types of investigations.

11. Especially helpful was Albert Mangones, architect and former director of the bureau of ethnology. He provided *Moin Pa Ou, Voisin,* and the explanation given herein.

12. The use of Spanish in Port-au-Prince is not surprising, given the proximity of the Dominican Republic. Note, however, the occasional occurrence of Spanish names in Guadeloupe.

13. Note again the mixing of Spanish and French.

14. This may, of course, commemorate a wife, daughter, or girl friend of the chauffeur. More likely, however, it is a reference to the Haitian folk song (actually a kind of morality) about the girl who can't wash and iron and who therefore must be returned to her mother.

15. In most cases, of course, where the official language is French, most of the populace speaks French Creole (often called 'patois'). Names, however, much more frequently are in Standard French – with an occasional bit of Creole interference. In English speaking areas, a partly decreolized version of English Creole is characteristic. Although Surinam has Dutch as its official language, the functional importance of English is reflected in the bus names:

OK Let's Go	India Star
Love Car	Shooting Star
Roy Taxi	Road Master
Jimmy's Comet	Flying Master
Flying Arrow	

I did not observe a single name, and none were reported to me, in Sranan Tongo, the English creole which is very slightly decreolized if at all. Heinz Eersel, then director of the Taalbureau, told me that there were such names in Hindustani.

16. See note 12.

17. According to informants, the owner of this vehicle was suspected of complicity in an incident in which a shot was fired from his Volkswagen. Presence of that Volkswagen, with that name, on the spot at the hour of the crime made his defense especially difficult.

18. Informants have given me different interpretations of this name. A Puerto Rican girl who has relatives in St. Croix and whose father is Creole-speaking Black, cites 'How's your baby shaft?' – a question to newlyweds about their sex life. A professor compares Shaft, a character in American detective movies, and invokes consonant cluster /-ft/ simplification to /-f/. My belief is that the owner probably punned upon those two and another suggested by Jamaican poet John Figueroa – Show Off.

19. A Walt Disney animated cartoon, 'The Love Bug', featured a Volkswagen hero and may have influenced the name. Sexual and personal allusion is, however, commonplace in Afro-American car naming practices. Syncretism of two traditions is probable.

20. DeCamp lists names like The Rocket, Sky Rocket, Radar, The Missile, The Uptown Contender Transport, Get There Today, Come Make Me Hold Yuh Hand, Spree Boy, Little Hero, Funny Man, Young Tiger, Tiger Boy, Baby Boy, Mambo Boy, Spitfire, Romeo, Rowdy, Happy Girl, Romance Girl, and Honey Love. He collected only one indisputably religious name: Christ Mercy.

21. This name, was seen by Professor Kenneth Johnson of the University of California, Berkeley, on a pink car which had a Black driver. *Titty pink,* as

a designation for almost any object which is unexpectedly pink, is of course a regular part of vernacular male American culture. To claim it for Black influence would be unwarranted, although of course the possibility cannot be discarded without being investigated. The same may be said of other usages, such as *motherfucker*.

22. See DeCamp, *op. cit.*, p. 21, points out that the name Tiger Boy was given because the owner 'always wished people would call' him that. DeCamp also finds 'a highly unusual outlet for personal expression' in such names as I am Lonely, Lonely Boy, Leave Me Alone, Remember Me, Don't Gamble With Love, Black and Hungry, Man on Spot, and Forget Me Not. He finds the Jamaican laborer 'carrying on heroically beneath a great load of misfortunes, sustaining himself with hard work and a sense of humor. This attitude appears in Little Hero, Little Hero's Daily Bread, The Toiling Boy, Bread and Butter, Daily Bread . . . and Jackson's Labour'.

23. There is, of course, considerable debate on this point. See the works of Stewart, Hancock, Dalby, and Dillard (Bibliography). As Stewart's 'Acculturative Processes and the Language of the American Negro' (forthcoming) details exceptionally well, the primary resistance to the notion that language and culture of the Black group in the United States can differ from those of the whites of the same region comes from scholars who hold an assimilationist interpretation of American history. Considerable resistance to that point of view is also offered in my *Perspectives on Black English* (Mouton, 1975) and *All-American English* (Random House, 1975).

24. Parrinder (1953) lists religious mottoes on houses, in English:

> God is God
> God be with you
> The Rock of Ebenezer
> God's gift, good luck
> etc.

There are six others in English, three in Latin, and 27 African language mottoes with translations like 'Glory to God' and 'God give me joy'.

25. University of Texas Press, 1962, p. 158. Biggers's book is noteworthy for its intelligent presentation of the experience of an American Black looking for West African roots. Besides that, its drawings are extremely interesting.

26. *Names* 14 (3) (September, 1966): 157–160. Price and Price assert: 'We have no doubt that a closer study of the significance of such canoe names, reported throughhout the Antilles, would reap rich ethnographic rewards.'

27. *Ibid.*, p. 158.

28. This is, obviously, not an objection to the practices of Price and Price. In fact, I believe that the opinions of these experienced fieldworkers in Afro-American communities are excellent corroboration of the intuitions expressed by others that these are in fact names.

29. The rather diffident name is reminiscent of Camerounian pushcarts (*En Lieu de Chomer*) and of some of the Jamaican pushcarts listed by Decamp (1960).

30. Price and Price, p. 157.

31. I am indebted to Paul Nybroek, a Surinam student at the University of Puerto Rico, for these names. The orthography is his own.

32. This is, of course the contracted form for *Mi E Doe* (I + continuous aspect + do).

33. Nybroek did not report as to whether these were even put into writing, but

it can probably be assumed that they were not.

34. I am indebted to Dr. Paul Baum, Colegio Universitario del Sagrado Corazon, for this list. Baum was also one of many (William A. Stewart, Morris Goodman, John Roy, John Figueroa, Heinz Eersel, Richard Allsopp, and Mervin Alleyne are others whose names come immediately to mind) with whom I have discussed the general Afro-American distribution of these and other names.

35. The *San Juan Star Magazine*, May 19, 1974, p. 3. This boat is identified as belonging to the Gumbs family, which is the familiar Afro-Caribbean version of the Portuguese name Gomes. On the importance of a variety of Portuguese in the development of Creole languages (including French and English Creoles) see Whinnom, 1965.

36. As in the West African Pidgin forms (see note 5) this probably translates as *Pam Is Civil* rather than as an imperative verb with noun of address: *Pam, Be Civil.*

37. Jamaican informants have told me that *stamp-and-go* is used for the type of lunch brought to a laborer who is working in the fields (usually by his wife or some other family member).

38. See especially Stewart, 'Acculturative Processes . . .' (forthcoming), and Peter Wood, *Black Majority*, 1974.

39. P. 277.

40. The same entry is designated a common noun in Gonzales's Glossary, p. 335. Proper noun to common noun is not at all uncommon as a grammatical development in Afro-American etymons. T. Petzoldt, of Paramaribo, Surinam, cited the case of a garbage truck which bore the name 100. Thereafter, he reported, such trucks were called 'Number 100' even if they bore no numbers.

41. *Laguerre, A Gascon of the Black Border*, 1924, p. 293.

42. Cf. also the use of *Cuffee* and the other day names as common nouns (De Camp 1967).

43. DeCamp 1960:22.

44. P. 123.

45. Mary Wheeler, *Steamboatin' Days*, 1944, p. 52.

46. Herbert Quick and Edward Quick, *Mississippi Steamboats*, 1926, p. 235 f.

47. Wheeler, p. 52.

48. Wheeler reports: 'There are many Stacker Lee songs. Some of them can be connected with the packet boat; others center around the personality of a lawless character who was known and feared along the Ohio until a conviction for murder put an end to his career about forty years ago' (p. 100). The Black folk song about Stagolee is of course very well known. See, for example, Courlander 1963: 177–179.

49. Quick and Quick, *op. cit.*, p. 250.

50. Wheeler, *op. cit.*, p. 210.

51. *Ibid.* Note the dialect, which is more authentic than some critics have been willing to allow. See my *Black English* and Stewart (forthcoming).

52. Wheeler, *op cit.*, p. 20. Wheeler also demonstrates a great deal of further relationship between steamboat names and Black American musical culture. She points out, for example, the relationship between The Golden City, built in 1876, and 'Oh Dem Golden Slippers', published in 1879. Furthermore, it appears that there was a song called 'Golden City' which dealt with the ship and which had a melody strikingly like that of the famous spiritual (p. 51). Quick and Quick, *op. cit.*, also call attention to the songs of the

Black roustabouts on the river boats:

Jes' look at 'Tobin's Train'
Her wheels is beatin' 'Juba' (p. 250).

NOTES TO CHAPTER 5: 'SHOPS, VENDORS, AND THINGS FOR SALE'

1. Besides the examples of slaves taking passengers from ships in the Jamaican *Tom Kringle's Log* (1833; see last chapter, including note 36), examples can be cited from sources like Alexander Mackay, *The Western World; or, Travels in the United States in 1846–1847*, p. 133.
2. Perhaps the most precise statement of such practices is to be found in Fogel and Engerman, *Time on the Cross*, p. 142:

   Garden patches were assigned to the husbands [in slave families] and the money earned from the sale of crops from these patches was held in his name. When slaves wanted advances of cash from these accounts, they were made to the men.

   See also pp. 151–152; Genovese 1974: 406–407, 535. For the Caribbean, see Goveia 1965: 238–9. Richard Price, 'Caribbean Fishing and Fishermen: A Historical Sketch', *American Anthropologist* 68 (1966) points out how 'Negro slaves, like their Indian predecessors, sold part of their catch for cash' (p. 1370).
3. A general survey of the economic conditions involved is given in E. Franklin Frazier, *Black Bourgeoisie*, 1957, Chapter I: 'The Roots of the Black Bourgeoisie'.
4. Although Pidgin (or Cameroonian Creole) is the lingua franca of Buea Town and of other parts of the West Cameroon (and even competes with French in the East Cameroun), these names are predictably in Standard English. Obviously, the store owner sets out to put his best linguistic foot forward in the case of the names. Although I have no data from Nigeria, Ghana, Liberia, Sierra Leone, etc., it is not difficult to predict that the same situation would obtain there also.
5. N. T. Keeney, 'The Winds of Freedom Stir a Continent,' *National Geographic*, Vol. 118 (3) (September, 1960): 303–359.
6. In spite of the fact that the official language of Fernando Poo was Spanish, during my visit in 1965 Pidgin English was pretty clearly the lingua franca of Santa Isabel. Perhaps the main reason was the influx of Nigerian workers. A question like '¿Habla español?' was likely to elicit the answer 'simo!'. In keeping with general West African practice, the smallest actually functional unit of currency, the *peseta*, was (like the five-franc note in the Cameroun) referred to as a 'dollar' /dala/. A few shop names were also in Pidgin English, including the following on a tailor shop:

   Try and See
   The Federal Tailor
   I Look to God

7. I am grateful to Charles Gibson, then a Peace Corps volunteer stationed in Nkongsamba, for this and other valuable information concerning these names.
8. 'Cart Names in Jamaica', *Names* VIII (1960): 17.

9. Compare DeCamp's (*op. cit.*) Mr. Burry Still Trying, although he specifically points out that the owner of the cart was not named Mr. Burry.
10. The accepted local explanation for this name is that the owner, a Captain Weeke, bought it with a ten thousand dollar windfall.
11. There is an interior spot in St. Croix which is called Barren Spot on the map.
12. Helen Jaskoski, 'Power Unequal to Man: The Significance of Conjure in Works by Five Afro-American Authors', *Southern Folklore Quarterly* XXXVIII (1974): 91. She defines it as 'that body of lore and wisdom which is African in origin and inspiration and therefore outside of and opposed to the dominant Anglo-American culture'.
13. *Hoodoo, Conjuration, Witchcraft, Rootwork,* Memoirs of the Alma Egan Hyatt Foundation, Vol. I (1970); Vol. II (1970); Vol. III (1973).
14. Vol. II, unnumbered appendix.
15. P. 4. There is also a significant anecdote about a boy who names the 'chief products of St. Thomas': Tantan seed, Jumbee bead and Maran.
16. See George Eaton Simpson, *The Shango Cult in Trinidad,* Institute of Caribbean Studies Monograph Series No. 2, 1965, particularly the list 'Materials used in Healing and Conjuring', pp. 64–68.
17 See my *Black English* (1972), Chapter V.
18. Hyatt, *op. cit.,* I:111.
19. In the United States, Hyatt's work and Peter Wood, *Black Majority,* 1974, are virtually the only such works which consider the situation seriously. There is, however, an extremely valuable perspective to be gained from the great numbers of ethnographic works done in the West Indies. Perhaps the diffidence of West Indian scholars keeps them from pointing out to continental U. S. researchers how much the latter are missing because they deprive themselves of the insights which are obvious from the perspective of the Caribbean. See Dillard 1964 for one attempt to call the attention of scholars in the United States to such a matter, specifically the insights to be gained from the West Indian work of Herskovits.
20. In many ways, one of the most healthful signs in recent work on the history of the United States has been the rash of works on Black history. There seems to be special value in books on the Blacks on the American frontier, like William Loren Katz's *The Black West* (1973). Katz's work is invaluable in correcting the imbalance of earlier historical works, which made American cowboys and frontiersmen lily white and Anglo-Saxon. The trouble is that, in their eagerness to portray Blacks on the frontier, Katz and others (Philip Durham and Everett L. Jones, *The Negro Cowboys,* 1965) say virtually nothing about whites on the frontier or about Black-white relationships. Thus, in correcting the obviously distorted picture of an American West peopled only by whites, they inadvertently create the opposite distortion of a presentation of Blacks all alone in the wilderness. Neither group ever does very much about the relations of both groups to the Indians, although we know that there were such contacts. A shining exception to the last flaw is the work of Kenneth Wiggins Porter, *The Negro on the American Frontier,* New York, 1970; 'Negro Guides and Interpreters in the Early Stages of the Seminole War', *The Journal of Negro History* XXV, 1960; 'Seminole Indian Scouts, 1870–1881', *The Southwestern Historical Quarterly,* 1952; etc. The Seminoles constitute the major exception to the rule that Negro-Indian relations on the American continent have not been investigated – have, indeed, been factored out of the historical picture. Unfortunately, there are very few studies of cultural transmission even

among the Seminoles. Perhaps the most complete study is Frances Densmore, *Seminole Music*, Washington, D.C. 1956.

21. Exceptions are Ricardo Alegría, *La Fiesta de Santiago Apostol en Loiza Aldea*, Madrid, 1954; and Manuel Álvarez Nazario, *El Elemento Afronegroïde en el Español de Puerto Rico*, San Juan, 1961. Pedro Escabí (ed.), *Morovis: Vista Parcial del Folklore de Puerto Rico*, Río Piedras, n.d., considers African elements and reasserts the influence of Indian culture on Puerto Rican popular culture. This viewpoint seems important, and not really contradictory to the principles of (e.g.) the American 'Creolists'. A selection of the common elements of disparate cultural patterns (or languages) in contact was obviously an important part of the large scale mixing which went on in the early history of the New World. In language terms, the mixing of dialects produced a *koiné* (see my *All-American English*, 1975) and the contact between a large number of languages facilitated the spread of (although I do not believe that it *created*) a Lingua Franca – Pidgin English.

22. Lawrence M. Davis, 'Social Dialectology in America: A Criticial Survey', *Journal of English Linguistics* IV (1971): 46–56. Davis specifically directs attention to 'the names he [an informant] used for, say, a pastry made from corn meal (*corn bread, johnny cake*, and dozens of others)' (p. 46).

23. For criticisms other than my own and those of Stewart, see Dennis R. Preston, 'Social Dialectology in America: A Critical Rejoinder', *Florida FL Reporter* Spring/Fall, 1972.

Bibliography

Adams, S. C. (1947), 'The acculturation of the delta Negro', *Social Forces* 26, 202–205. Reprinted in Dundes, 1973.

Alegría, Ricardo (1954), *La Fiesta de Santiago Apostol en Loiza Aldea*, Madrid.

Algeo, John (1973), *On Defining the Proper Name*, Gainesville, Florida.

Álvarez Nazario, Manuel (1961), *El Elemento Afronegroïde en el Español de Puerto Rico*, San Juan.

Anonymous (1891), 'Word shadows', *Atlantic Monthly* LXVII, 143–144. Reprinted in Jackson, 1967.

Atkins, John (1735), *A Voyage to Guinea, Brazil, and the West Indies*, London.

Attaway, William (1952), *Calypso Song Book*, London.

Bailey, Charles-J. N. (1974), 'Review of Dillard, *Black English*', *Foundations of Language* 11.

Barth, Ernest A. T. (1961), 'The language behavior of Negroes and whites', *Pacific Sociological Review* IV, 69–72.

Bascom, William R. (1941), 'Acculturation among the Gullah Negroes', *American Anthropologist* 43, 43–50. Reprinted in J. L. Dillard (ed.), *Perspectives on Black English*, The Hague, Mouton, 1975.

Beck, Robert ('Iceberg Slim') (1967), *Pimp: The Story of My Life*, Los Angeles.

Biggers, John (1962), *Ananse, The Web of Life in Africa*, Austin, Texas.

'Black Names' (1968), *Newsweek* LXII (July 29), 80.

Blesh, Rudi and Harriet Janis (1950), *They All Played Ragtime*, New York.

Bourgignon, Erika (1970), 'Ritual dissociation and possession belief in Caribbean Negro religion', in Norman Whitten and John Szwed (eds.), *Afro-American Anthropology: Contemporary Perspectives*, New York.

Cassidy, Frederic G. (1957), 'Iteration as a word-forming device in Jamaican folk speech', *American Speech XXXII*, 49–53.

— (1961), *Jamaica Talk; Three Hundred Years of the English Language in Jamaica*, London.

Cassidy, Frederic G., and David DeCamp (1966), 'Names for an albino among Jamaica Negroes', *Names* 14, 129–133.

Charters, Samuel (collector) (1964), *The Rural Blues, Record, Book, and Film Sales, Inc.*, New York.

Cohen, John (1965), 'The folk music interchange', *Sing Out!* Dec. 1964 – Jan. 1965.

Courlander, Harold (1963), *Negro Folk Music, U.S.A.* New York, Columbia University Press.

Crow, Captain Hugh (1791), *Memoirs*, London.

Dalby, David (1972), 'The African element in American English', in Kochman (ed.), *Rappin' and Stylin' Out: Communication in Urban Black America*, Urbana, University of Illinois Press.

Davis, Lawrence (1969), 'Dialect research: Mythology versus reality', *Orbis* XVIII, 332–337.

Davis, Lawrence (1971), 'Social dialectology in America: A critical rejoinder', *Journal of English Linguistics* IV, 46–56.

DeCamp, David (1960), 'Cart names in Jamaica', *Names* VIII.

— (1967), 'African day names in Jamaica', *Language* 43, 130–147.

de Granda, Germán (1971), 'Testimónios documentales sobre la preservación del sistema antroponimico twi entre los esclavos negros de la Nueva Grenada', *Revista Española de la Lingüistica* I, 265–274.

Deutsch, Cynthia (1964), 'Auditory discrimination and learning: Social factors', *Merrill-Palmer Quarterly* X, 274–296.

Dillard, J. L. (1963), *Afro-American and Other Vehicle Names*, Special Study No. 1, Institute of Caribbean Studies, Río Piedras, University of Puerto Rico.

— (1964), 'The writings of Herskovits and the study of the language of the Negro in the New World', *Caribbean Studies*.

— (1968), 'On the grammar of Afro-American naming practices', *Names* XVI, 230–237.

— (1971), 'The West African day names in Nova Scotia', *Names* XIX, 257–261.

— (1972a), *Black English; Its History and Usage in the United States*, New York.

— (1972b), 'Afro-American, Spanglish, and something else: St. Cruzan naming practices', *Names* XX, 225–230.

— (1973), 'The history of Black English in Nova Scotia', *African Language Review* 9, 263–279.

— (ed.) (1975a), *Perspectives on Black English*, The Hague, Mouton.

— (1975b), *All-American English, A History of American English*, New York.

Donald, Henderson H. (1952), *The Negro Freedman*, New York.

Dundes, Alan (ed.) (1973), *Mother Wit from the Laughing Barrel*, Englewood Cliffs, New Jersey.

Edwards, Bryan (1807), Observations on the disposition, character, manners, and habits of life of the Maroon Negroes on the island of Jamaica', in *The History of the West Indies*, London 1807 I, 537–545. Reprinted in Richard Price (ed.), *Maroon Societies*, Garden City, New York, 1973.

Ellison, Ralph (1952), *The Invisible Man*, New York.

Escabí, Pedro C. (n.d.), *Morovis: Vista Parcial del Folklore de Puerto Rico*, Río Piedras.

Ewen, David (1964), *The Life and Death of Tin Pan Alley*, New York.

Fader, Daniel (1971), *The Naked Children*, New York.

Fairclough, G. Thomas (1960), ' "New light" on "old Zion" ', *Names*.

Fauset, Arthur Huff (1938), *Sojourner Truth – God's Faithful Pilgrim*, Chapel Hill, North Carolina.

Fergusson, C. G. (1948), *A Documentary Study of the Establishment of Negroes in Nova Scotia Between the War of 1812 and the Winning of Responsible Government*, Public Archives of Nova Scotia.

Fickett, Joan (1972), *Aspects of Morphemics, Syntax, and Semology of an Inner-City Dialect (Merican)*, West Rush, New York.

Fisher, Miles Mark (1953), *Negro Slave Songs in the United States*, New York.

Fogel, Robert William, and Stanley L. Engerman (1974), *Time on the Cross; The Economics of Negro Slavery*, New York.

Frazier, E. Franklin (1957), *Black Bourgeoisie*, New York.
Genovese, Eugene (1975), *Roll, Jordan, Roll; The World the Slaves Made*, New York.
Gonzales, Ambrose (1922), *The Black Border; Gullah Stories of the Carolina Coast*, Columbia, South Carolina.
— (1924), *Laguerre: A Gascon of the Black Border*, Columbia, South Carolina.
Goveia, Elsa (1965), *Slave Society in the British Leeward Islands at the End of the Eighteenth Century*, Institute of Caribbean Studies, Río Piedras.
Grade, P. (1892) 'Das Neger-Englisch an der west küste von Afrika', *Anglia* XIV, 362–393.
Greene, Lorenzo Johnston (1942), *The Negro in Colonial New England, 1620–1776*, Columbia University Studies in History, Economics, and Public Law No. 494.
Gunther, John (1953), *Inside Africa*, New York.
Hannerz, Ulf (1968), 'The rhetoric of soul', *Race* IX, 453–465.
— (1969), *Soulside: Inquiries into Ghetto Culture and Community*, New York.
Hellman, John M., Jr. (1973) ' "I'm a Monkey": The influence of the Black American blues argot on the Rolling Stones', *Journal of American Folklore* 86: 367–373.
Hentoff, Nat and Albert McCarthy (1959), *Jazz*, New York.
Herskovits, Melville J. (1958), *The Myth of the Negro Past*, Boston.
— 1966, 'What has Africa given America?' in Frances S. Herskovits (ed.), *The New World Negro*, Bloomington, Indiana.
— (1937), *Life in a Haitian Valley*, New York.
— (1938), *Dahomey, An Ancient West African Kingdom*, New York.
Herskovits, Melville J., and Francis Herskovits (1936), 'Suriname Folk-Lore', *Columbia Contributions to Anthropology*, Vol. 27.
Hoetink, Harmannus (1962), ' "Americant" in Samaná, *Caribbean Studies*.
Hogg, Donald (1966), 'Statement of a Ras Tafari leader', *Caribbean Studies*.
Hughes, Langston (1960), *An African Treasury*, New York.
Hughes, Langston, and Milton Meltzner (1967), *Black Magic, A Pictorial History of the Negro in American Entertainment*, New York.
Hyatt, Harry Middleton (1970), *Hoodoo, Conjuration, Witchcraft, Rootwork, Memoirs of the Alma Egan Hyatt Foundation*, Vols. I and II.
— (1973), *Hoodoo, Conjuration, Witchcraft, Rootwork, Memoirs of the Alma Egan Hyatt Foundation*, Vol. III.
Jackson, Bruce (1965), 'Prison folklore', *Journal of American Folklore* LXXVIII, 317–329.
— (ed.) (1967), *The Negro and His Folklore in Nineteenth-Century Periodicals*, American Folklore Society.
Jeremiah, Milford A. (forthcoming), 'The Linguistic Relatedness of Black English and Antiguan Creole', Brown University dissertation.
Johnson, Kenneth R. (1973), 'Words used for skin color in the Black culture', *Florida FL Reporter* 11 (1 and 2).
Jones, LeRoi (1963), *Blues People*, New York.
Kelley, William Melvyn (1968), *Dunford's Travels Everywhere*, New York.
Keeney, F. N. (1960), 'The winds of freedom stir a continent', *National Geographic* 118: 303–359.
Keil, Charles (1966), *The Urban Blues*, New York.
Kiner, Henry A. (1962), 'Old Corn Meal: A forgotten urban Negro folksinger', *Journal of American Folklore* 75: 29–34.
Kochman, Thomas (ed.) (1972), *Rappin' and Stylin' Out: Communication in Ur-*

ban Black America, Urbana, University of Illinois Press.

Kohl, Herbert and James Hinton (1972), 'Names, graffiti, and culture', in Kochman (ed.), *Rappin' and Stylin' Out*, Urbana, University of Illinois Press.

Labov, William (1972), *Language in the Inner City*, Philadelphia.

Labov, William, Paul Cohen, and Clarence Robins (1965), *A Preliminary Study of the Structure of English Used by Negro and Puerto Rican Speakers in New York City*, New York.

Labov, William, Paul Cohen, Clarence Robins, and John Lewis (1968), *A Study of the Non-Standard English of Negro and Puerto Rican Speakers in New York City*, U. S. Office of Education Cooperative Research Project No. 3288.

Liebow, Elliot (1967), *Talley's Corner: A Study of Negro Streetcorner Men*, Boston.

Loflin, Marvin D. (1967), 'A note on the deep structure of nonstandard English in Washington, D. C.', *Glossa* I, 26–32.

— (1969), 'On the passive in nonstandard Negro English', *Journal of English as a Second Language* IV, 19–23.

— (1975), 'Black American English and syntactic dialectology', in J. L. Dillard (ed.), *Perspectives on Black English*, The Hague, Mouton.

Lomax, Alan (1950), *Mr. Jelly Roll*, New York.

Lomax, Ruby T. (1943), 'Negro nicknames', *Texas Folklore Society Bulletin* XVIII, 163–171.

Mackay, Alexander (1850), *The Western World; or Travels in the United States in 1846–1847*, London.

McCormack, Mack (1958), 'Lightnin' Hopkins: Blues', in Martin Williams (ed.), *Jazz Panorama*, New York.

— (collector), *A Treasury of Field Recordings*, 77 Records 77-LA-12-3.

McCullers, Carson Smith (1940), *The Heart Is a Lonely Hunter*, Boston.

Manning, Frank E. (1974), 'Nicknames and number plates in the British West Indies', *Journal of American Folklore* 87: 123–132.

McDavid, Raven I., Jr. (1967), 'Historical, regional, and social variation', *Journal of English Linguistics* I.

Mellers, Wilfrid (1966), *Music in a New Found Land; Themes and Developments in the History of American Music*, New York.

Mencken, H. L. (1919), *The American Language*, First edition, New York.

Métraux, Alfred (1971), 'Cooperative labor groups in Haiti', in Michael Horowitz (ed.), *Peoples and Cultures of the Caribbean*, Natural History Press.

Mezzrow, Milton 'Mezz' (1946), *Really The Blues*, New York.

Middleton, Richard (1972), *Pop Music and the Blues*, London.

Morrison, Toni (1974), *Sula*, New York.

Nathan, Hans (1962), *Dan Emmett and the Rise of Early Negro Minstrelsy*, Norman, Oklahoma.

Noreen, R. S. (1965), 'Ghetto worship: A study of Chicago store front churches', *Names* XIII, 19–38.

Odum, Howard W., and Guy B. Johnson (1926), *Negro Workaday Songs*, Chapel Hill, North Carolina.

Oliver, Paul (1963) *The Meaning of the Blues*, New York.

— (1970), *Aspects of the Blues Tradition*, New York.

Olmsted, Frederic Law (1861), *A Journey in the Back Country*, New York.

Panassie, Hugues, and Madeleine Gautier (1956), *A. Guide to Jazz*, Boston.

Parrinder, Geoffrey (1953), *Religion in an African City*, Oxford University Press.

Peterson, Arona (1974), *Herbs and Proverbs of the Virgin Islands*, St. Thomas.

Pickford, Glenna Ruth (1956), 'American linguistic geography: A sociological appraisal", *Word.* Reprinted in Dillard (ed.), *Perspectives on Black English.*
Preston, Dennis R. (1972), 'Social dialectology in America: A critical rejoinder', *Florida FL Reporter,* Spring/Fall.
Price, Richard (1966), 'Caribbean fishing and fishermen: A historical sketch', *American Anthropologist* 68.
— (ed.) (1973), *Maroon Societies,* Garden City, New York.
Price, Richard, and Sally Price (1966), 'A note on canoe names in Martinique', *Names* XIV, 157–160.
— (1972), 'Saramaka onomastics: An Afro-American naming practice', *Ethnology* XI, 341–367.
Puckett, Newbell Niles (1937), 'Names of American Negro slaves', in George P. Murdock (ed.), *Studies in the Science of Society,* New Haven, Yale University Press.
Quick, Herbert, and Edward Quick (1926), *Mississippi Steamboats.*
Ramsey, Frederic (1960), *Been Here and Gone,* Brunswick, New Jersey.
Ramsey, Frederic, and Charles Edward Smith (1939) *Jazzmen,* New York.
Reed, Ishmael (1974), *The Last Days of Louisiana Red,* New York.
Reisner, Robert George (1959), *The Jazz Titans,* Garden City, New York.
Russell, Tony (1970), *Blacks, Whites, and the Blues,* New York.
Saxon, Lyle (1945), *Gumbo Ya-Ya, A Collection of Louisiana Folk Tales,* Boston.
Schneider, Gilbert D. (1963), *First Steps in Wes-Kos,* Hartford Connecticut.
— (1965), *Wes-Kos Proverbs, Idioms, Names,* Preliminary Copy.
Schuller, Gunther (1968), *Early Jazz,* New York.
Shapiro, Nat, and Nat Hentoff (1957), *The Jazz Makers,* New York.
Simpson, George Eaton (1965), *The Shango Cult in Trinidad,* Institute of Caribbean Studies Monograph Series No. 2.
Slonimsky, Nicholas (1971), *Music Since 1900,* Fourth edition, New York.
Smith, Charles Edward (1959), 'New Orleans and traditions in jazz', in Nat Hentoff and Albert McCarthy, *Jazz,* New York.
Smith Elsdon (1969), *American Surnames,* Philadelphia.
Stearns, Marshall (1956), *The Story of Jazz,* New York.
Stearns, Marshall, and Jean Stearns (1966), 'Frontiers of humor: American vernacular dance', *Southern Folklore Quarterly,* 227–235.
— (1968), *Jazz Dance,* New York.
Stewart, William A. (1964), 'Urban Negro speech: Sociolinguistic factors affecting English teaching', in Shuy (ed.), *Social Dialects and Language Learning,* NCTE.
— (1967), 'Sociolinguistic factors in the history of American Negro dialects', *Florida FL Reporter.*
— (1968), 'Continuity and change in American Negro dialects', *Florida FL Reporter.*
— (1970), 'Sociopolitical issues in the linguistic issues in the linguistic treatment of Negro dialect', *Report of the Twentieth Round Table,* Washington, D.C., Georgetown University.
— (forthcoming), 'Acculturative processes and the language of the American Negro', in William Gage (ed.), *Language in Its Social Setting,* Washington, D.C..
Stowe, Harriet Beecher (1853), *The Key to Uncle Tom's Cabin,* London.
— (1863), 'Sojourner Truth, the Libyan Sibyl', *Atlantic Monthly,* 473–481.
Stronks, James B. (1964), 'Chicago store front churches: 1964', *Names* XII, 127–128.

Sutton, Horace (1971), Column in *Chicago Tribune*.
Scott, Michael (1833), *Tom Kringle's Log*, Edinburgh.
Turner, Lorenzo Dow (1949), *Africanisms in the Gullah Dialect*, Chicago.
Tucker, Nathaniel Beverly (1836), *The Partisan Leader*, Washington, D.C.
Underwood, Gary (1974), 'Dialect research in the Southwest', *International Journal of the Sociology of Language* 2.
Voorhoeve, Jan (1973), 'Historical and linguistic evidence in favour of the relexification theory in the formation of Creoles', *Language in Society* 2, 133–146.
Wheeler, Mary (1944), *Steamboatin' Days, Folk Songs of the River Packet Era*, Baton Rouge, Louisiana.
Whinnom, Keith (1965), 'The origin of the European-based pidgins and creoles', *Orbis*.
Whitten, Norman (1962), 'Contemporary patterns of malign occultism among Negroes in North Carolina', *Journal of American Folklore* 75: 311–325. Reprinted in Dundes (ed.), *Mother Wit from the Laughing Barrel*, 1973.
Whitten, Norman, and John Szwed (eds.) (1970), *Afro-American Anthropology: Contemporary Perspectives*, New York.
Williams, Martin T. (ed.) (1959) *The Art of Jazz*, New York.
— (1964), *Jazz Panorama*, New York.
Wood, Peter (1974), *Black Majority*, New York.
Yetman, Norman R. (1970), *Life Under the 'Peculiar Institution': Selections from the Slave Narrative Collection*, New York.

CONTRIBUTIONS TO THE SOCIOLOGY OF LANGUAGE

Edited by Joshua A. Fishman

1. *Advances in the Sociology of Language*
   Volume I: Basic Concepts, Theories and Problems: Alternative
   Approaches
   Ed. by J. A. Fishman
   1976, 418 pages, 2nd ed. Clothbound
   ISBN: 90-279-7732-1

2. *Advances in the Sociology of Language*
   Volume II: Selected Studies and Applications
   Ed. by J. A. Fishman
   1972, 534 pages. Paperbound
   ISBN: 90-279-2302-7

3. *Multilingualism in the Soviet Union*
   Aspects of Language Policy and its Implementation
   by E. Glyn Lewis
   1972, xx + 332 pages. Paperbound
   ISBN: 90-279-2352-3

4. *Perspectives on Black English*
   Ed. by J. L. Dillard
   1975, 392 pages. Clothbound
   ISBN: 90-279-7811-5

5. *Advances in Language Planning*
   Ed. by J. A. Fishman
   1974, 590 pages. Paperbound
   ISBN: 90-279-2618-2

6. *The Revival of a Classical Tongue*
   Eliezer Ben Yehuda and the Modern Hebrew Language
   by Jack Fellman
   1973, 152 pages. Paperbound
   ISBN: 90-279-2495-3

7. *The Political Sociology of the English Language*
   An African Perspective (Who are the Afro-Saxons?)
   by Ali A. Mazrui
   1975, 232 pages. Clothbound
   ISBN: 90-279-7821-2

CONTRIBUTIONS TO THE SOCIOLOGY OF LANGUAGE

Edited by Joshua A. Fishman

8. *Advances in the Creation and Revision of Writing Systems*
   Ed. by J. A. Fishman
   1976, in prep. Clothbound
   ISBN: 90-279-7552-3

9. *Advances in the Study of Societal Multilingualism*
   Ed. by J. A. Fishman
   1976, in prep. Clothbound
   ISBN: 90-279-7742-9

10. *Language and Politics*
    Ed. by William M. O'Barr and Jean F. O'Barr
    1976, in prep. Clothbound
    ISBN: 90-279-7761-5

11. *Universalism versus Relativism in Language and Thought*
    Proceedings of a Colloquium on the Sapir — Whorf Hypothesis
    Ed. by Rik Pinxten
    1976, in prep. Clothbound
    ISBN: 90-279-7791-7

12. *Selection among Alternatives in Language Standardization*
    The Case of Albanian
    by Janet Byron
    1976, 160 pages. Paperbound
    ISBN: 90-279-7542-6

13. *Language Planning for Modernization*
    The Case of Indonesian and Malaysian
    by S. Takdir Alisjabana
    1976, in prep. Paperbound
    ISBN: 90-279-7712-7

14. *Issues in Sociolinguistics*
    Ed. by R. O. J. Uribe-Villegas
    1976, in prep. Clothbound
    ISBN: 90-279-7722-4

Other volumes are in preparation

MOUTON · THE HAGUE · PARIS